DATE DUE

GAYLORD			PRINTED IN U.S.A.

The Use of Life

Life has been lent to us, and we owe it to our traveling-companions to let them see what use we make of it to the end. We must show our brethren both how to live and how to die.

He who asks of life nothing but the improvement of his own nature, and a continuous moral progress toward inward contentment and religious submission, is less liable than any one else to miss, and waste life.

HENRI FRÉDERIC AMIEL (1821-1881)

The Use of Life

FREDERICK WARD KATES, 1910 —

HARPER & BROTHERS — NEW YORK

For
R. C. K.
Who Showed Me the Use of Life
and for
Elizabeth, William and Thomas

This is the best of me; for the rest, I ate, and drank, and slept, and loved, and hated, like another; my life was as the vapor and is not; but this I saw and knew; this, if anything of mine, is worth your memory.

Sir Edward Elgar (1857-1934)
at the end of original manuscript of
his oratorio "The Dream of Gerontius"

CONTENTS

Introductory: *The Key Decision*

What are you going to do with your life? What use are you going to make of it?

The answer to these questions, whether made at twenty or forty, constitutes for everyone the key decision of life. It is even more fateful than the choice of one's partner in marriage or deciding not to marry at all. And it is, actually, no less serious a concern for a person in the midstream of life than for the young person standing on the threshold of adult experience.

Of course, one can make no particular issue of the matter: one can just drift through the years until life is done. But this is impossible for the person who wants to get the most out of life and who also wants to make a contribution to it. For the person who prefers to live, not just vegetate, the decision regarding the use of life is the major one of a lifetime.

William James, in a letter written to his mother in 1863 at the age of twenty-one, discloses a realization of what we mean. "I feel very much the importance of making soon a final choice of my business in life," wrote the young man destined to become one of America's foremost psychologists.

"I stand now at the place where the road forks. One branch leads to material comfort, the fleshpots, but it seems a kind of selling one's soul. The other leads to mental dignity and independence, combined, however, with physical penury. . . . I fear there might be some anguish in looking back from the pinnacle of prosperity (necessarily reached, if not by eating dirt, at least by renouncing some divine ambrosia) over the life you might have led in the pure pursuit of truth. It seems as if one could not afford to give that up for any bribe, however great."

Not all people, by any means, are enthralled by the prospect of spending life "in the pure pursuit of truth." Only a rare few are so attracted. Far more people consider the highest use to which life can be devoted is the accumulation of money, property, and possessions. Others seem to think that the supreme use of life is to satisfy, at all risks and at any cost, every selfish whim and desire and to indulge with unrestrained abandon every passion and instinct and appetite. To others the main purpose of life is to have as gay a time as they can as long as they are able. Still others appear to believe the chief use of life is to have one's name constantly in the newspaper headlines, to be conspicuous and great, if only for a day, in the eyes of men. But there are still others who are convinced that the highest use of life lies in other directions.

These folk are conscious of the unutterable preciousness of life, of what a wonderful thing it is just to be alive, and they are resolved to use this gift of life to its fullest capacity. They perfectly understand and immediately sympathize with the point of view of a man like Bishop Charles Henry Brent who wrote, a generation ago, "We can live this life but once . . . and it is only common sense to live it for all that it is worth, and in a way that would count even if death were to close accounts forever. If it is a thing of value and of power, let us test its capacity to the breaking-point and to the finish."

We may count these people softheaded romanticists or ivory-tower idealists, intending by so labeling them to damn them. But, however we choose to regard them, the fact remains that they are the people who are making the best possible use of the gift of life that God has granted them.

Just how, specifically, do these people think a man should spend his days? According to them, what is the proper and the best use of life?

The pages that follow are written to give the answer to these questions.

The Use of Life

1. Make Your Dream Come True

The person who has made up his mind that life is both too short and too wondrous a gift to waste in chasing after the baubles that other men value highly considers the great, overarching use of life is to spend his days making his dream come true. God, he believes, did not intend a man to crawl through his years like a grubbing insect to die unknown and unsung. Rather, God grants a man life that he may use it to make his dream come true.

Of course, there are hosts of men who neither hold nor are held by some overmastering dream that they want, above all else in life, to translate into fact. But for the man who is held captive by some mighty purpose or some exalted ambition life has no more important use than for the realization of that dream.

"It is our prerogative to be dreamers," Michael Fairless reminds us; therefore, we say, let us dare to dream. All great men have been, all great men are, dreamers: great men know dreams and follow them. From the time of Alexander of Macedon dreaming of the world under his thumb to our own day with the men in the Kremlin dreaming of the world under their iron rule, this has been so. Conquerors, adventurers, explorers, poets, statesmen, artists, scientists, and teachers, they are all men of dreams. And it was only nineteen hundred years ago that there walked this earth a man "of absolute beauty" who dreamed the noblest dream that has ever haunted the mind of man, the vision of the Kingdom of God among men.

"We grow great by dreams," Woodrow Wilson once said, and he might have added that we grow great by the discipline and suffering we are willing to undergo in seeking to make them come true. There is hardly a man who has not harbored in his heart some great dream or dreams, but for most men these shining visions have remained just dreams and for one reason or another they have never been realized. Very likely the fault lies in ourselves, for generally we are not brave enough to combat, or strong enough to overcome, the obstacles life throws in the pathway of making our dreams come to pass. Too frail are we to pursue the visions our eyes have seen.

Yet, while some of us allow these visions of something great and fine to come to nothing, there are others who "nourish and protect them, nurse them through bad days, till they bring them to the sunshine and light which come always to those who sincerely hope that their dreams will come true." These people who do not permit their dreams to fade away into vacant air have found that one of the paramount values of religion is that it helps them to keep their footing on the heights of their dreams.

So we urge every man to remain true to the dream that lights his days, be it a dream of writing a poem that for centuries to come will warm the hearts of men, of finding a cure for a cruel disease that now tortures mankind, or of helping in some humble way to establish more perfectly the reign of God's will and love and law among men. Hold fast to your dream whatever it may be, we press on every man, for who cherishes in his heart a vision of something high and great treads a magic pathway through all his years and finds that life is unfailingly an exciting adventure, free of boredom and full of melody and color.

To him who is reluctant to live in this fashion, we say: do not be afraid to devote your life to a search for some Holy Grail just because it is following an ideal which seems too distant ever to be attained. Every man knows that "life without pursuit is a vain and languid thing." It reduces to this: there are both a coward and a hero in the breast of every man and which a man shall be is for him alone to choose. Surely it is one of the supreme glories of manhood for a man to know that it is in his power to live, and if need be to die, for a vision of things to come, of a new world yet to be in the shaping of which he played a role, however modest.

Be not afraid to aim at a star. Such is our word to the timid in heart. We hit only what we aim at. Granted that we may miss the mark, at least when our arrow falls, it will be sheathed in flame. The ideal is the heritage of every man, not just certain chosen men, and the ideal is every man's to aspire for and to serve. In the service of the highest freedom and joy are supremely to be found. Life, to be rich and rewarding, has to be lived according to some splendid vision, some noble ideal, some magnificent dream. The vision that fills one's eyes gives life its meaning, its color, and its power. It is only the star caught in our eyes, it is only the dream we hold, or rather the dream that holds us, that matters.

Finally, this is true: dreams never die, though we on our part may be unfaithful to them and though we betray them. We live on our dreams, and for them, and by them. And a dream, in all its gossamer airiness, is stronger by far than the raw, rough sharpness of earth's harsh realities. Life, after all, is but our attempt to live our dreams.

"Our life is woven wind," Joseph Joubert once remarked. We weave threads of various hues and textures together to make the fabric that is our life. In Shakespeare's words, "The web of our life is of a mingled yarn, good and ill together." Through "the web of our life" we must keep the pattern, that is, our vision or our dream, or live and die disappointed and frustrated men.

Whether life will be an exciting romance to its closing hour or a dismal tale of humdrum existence depends on our willingness to stake all to make our dreams come true, lies in the risks we are willing to take for the sake of our ideals. If we are courageous enough to pay the price that is required to live our lives as chances to make our dreams come true, we shall discover what Thoreau learned as the result of his experiment of living alone at Walden Pond. This wise artist in living wrote: "I learned this, at least, by my experiment: that if one advances confidently in the direction of his dreams, and endeavors to live the life which he has imagined, he will meet with a success unexpected in common hours."

Yes, the whole of life lies in the risk we are willing to take and the price we are willing to pay to make our dreams come true. The only real failure in life is not to be true to the highest we know, and life's greatest victory is to persist undaunted in loyalty to our dream, seeking through the days of our years to make it come true. The one thing that gives life dignity and beauty and stature, lifts it out of mediocrity, saves it from futility and insignificance, and makes it worth-while in the end, is to have opened our eyes upon the highest, to have caught a vision of the best, to have had God's hand laid upon our shoulder and point our eyes to the stars, and then with all our strength, midst failures and faults, to have stood steadfast seeking to make our dream come true.

2. *Spend Life for Something That Will Outlast It*

If our first answer to the question, How best to use life? is to employ it in trying to make our dream come true, the second is stated for us by William James: "The great use of life is to spend it for something that will outlast it." Since a man has only one life and that for not very long at best, what better use for it is there than to dedicate it to the advancement of something that will continue beyond it? After all and with all angles of the matter considered, is it not preferable to serve something big and lasting even in a small way than something petty and transitory in a big way?

A memorable sentence by the late George Bernard Shaw comes to mind: "This is the true joy in life, the being used for a purpose recognized by yourself as a mighty one; the being thoroughly worn out before you are thrown on the scrap heap; the being a force of Nature instead of a feverish little clod of ailments and grievances complaining that the world will not devote itself to making you happy."

Is not this a splendid way to use life and the sensible way, "to spend it for something that will outlast it"? Is not this the fittest way for a man to use his gifts and talents and strength, "for a purpose recognized by yourself as a mighty one"?

What happiness is, no person can say for another, of course, but there have not been many in this world who have found happiness by living for themselves alone. The joy of living and joy in living come from dedication to, or immersion in, something we know to be bigger and better, finer and higher, more enduring and worthier, than we ourselves. "People, ideas, causes, above all, continuities, these offer the one possible escape not merely from selfishness but from the hungers of solitude and the sorrows of aimlessness," John Mason Brown has written. "Existence is a strange bargain," he continues. "Life owes us little; we owe it everything. The only true happiness comes from squandering ourselves for a purpose."

How best to use life? William James, George Bernard Shaw, and John Mason Brown each in turn supply us with the answer: to spend it for a purpose that is vastly bigger than ourselves and that will outlast our own short lives. To use life for anything less, to spend such a glorious gift as life in any lesser way, seems to the man who wants his life to count, irreverent, ignoble, and, at bottom, foolish.

If life's primary use is to spend our days and strength in seeking to make our dream come true, then the more exalted our dream and the nobler our purpose the better. Serving great causes, dedicating oneself to a magnificent purpose, this is what makes a man noble and great. Big purposes make big men and translating mighty dreams into facts brings out manhood in all its splendor. Small-scale dreams that are easily and readily realized do not stretch our muscles and impart to our lives stature and power. It is only a big dream of some goal high and fine and good and the endeavor to make it come true that raise a man's life above that of his fellows and lend it dignity and worth and meaning.

A purpose bigger than ourselves and our pigmy ambitions, a goal to aim at and a cause to serve that will outlast our own brief lives, where is such to be found?

Our answer is this: in the service of those things that permanently abide beyond our lives and that endure above time, the eternal values, goodness, truth, beauty, honor, justice, mercy, kindness, love, and good will among men.

If we live for this life only, for its baubles and bubbles, for its passing pleasures and transient joys, we shall end up bitterly disappointed men and women, and we shall find life hardly worth the price we have to pay to live it. In satisfactions of the body, in terms of this life and of this world, no man can ever know sufficient compensation. Be sure of this: if we live for the things of this world only, we shall live and die grievously frustrated people. Animals may live so, but not creatures fashioned in the image of God.

However, if we set our minds and our affections on things above, not on things of this earth, we shall find life intensely worth living and we shall escape boredom and a sense of pointlessness and futility. This earth, this life, this world and all the things thereof, pass away, but goodness and truth and beauty and love endure everlastingly. God and the things of God alone forever abide. If we dedicate our lives to the service of the things that are eternal, life is furnished with a purpose which glorifies even the most humdrum duties and puts a song into the drabbest of days and saddest of events.

Standing up for freedom and the liberty of men is to provide our lives with a majestic purpose which will outlive and outlast them. Every generation is called upon to take up the struggle on behalf of freedom, for freedom is not a prize that once won is possessed forever. Seemingly secured, freedom slips out of our grasp unless we are constantly vigilant and zealous in its protection. Not only shall we be girding our lives with a glorious purpose by defending freedom in our time, but we shall also be keeping faith with those who in years past have given and in the present are giving their devotion and lives for the same end.

A goal to work for and a cause to serve that will outlast our own brief lives, where is such to be found?

Supremely, we answer, in the service of that exciting enterprise Jesus of Nazareth came to earth to inaugurate and to establish among men, the reign of God's love and law and will.

Here is a purpose for a man's life that is in truth a mighty one, the Kingdom of God, the dominion of God's law and love in the affairs of men. Here, for sure, is a cause bigger and better, more enduring and worthier, than we are ourselves. Here is an objective to serve that will outlast our transitory lives. Here is something worth struggling for and suffering for with all that we have and are.

The Reign of God, its service and its glory, is the supremely worth-while use for our lives. If we hesitate to agree, then, we ask, What greater end or nobler goal can a man use his life to forward? What more exalted purpose can appeal to a man for his life allegiance?

Not only the hero but also any man who wants his life to count must dedicate his life to the loyal service of what eternally endures. Men find their lives and realize them most fully, not in sheltering and protecting them, but in using them to foster what is everlastingly worth living and worth dying for.

3. Work for a Better Tomorrow than Today

An obvious use of life to every man of a good will is to work with all his power to make today better than yesterday, tomorrow better than today. Every man of good will in the course of his life wants to have done something, however modest and unpretentious, to make the world a better place, a mite happier a place to live in, one notch closer to the ideal of the Kingdom of God. He wants to live in such wise that the world, after he has gone, is a fairer place for his having lived. This real, though often unspoken, desire of every man of a good heart is a paramount use of life: to live in such a way that tomorrow's world will be an improvement over today's.

Most men have a sincere desire to leave the world better than they found it and fondly hope that their lives may have contributed in some small measure to this end. There are, of course, many completely selfish people whose sole interest in life is the satisfaction of their appetites and of their lusts for self-advancement and power. They have no interest at all in the world that is to be. But a man at his best wants a better world for his children than the world he knew. A man at his best is not content to leave things as they are or worse than he found them: he wants, if possible, to leave them genuinely better.

But how? What can a man do toward making tomorrow better than today?

First of all, he can by every resource at his command seek to relieve the world's misery, its sorrow and its pain. While many of us cannot do much directly toward this end, no one of us will be excused from not doing what little he can. Directly and indirectly if that is the only way, we are bound, you and I, to relieve, to mitigate, and to remove the burden of mankind's suffering and sorrow and sin. Everyone who is engaged in any work of service whose object is the relief of humanity's agony and pain is playing a real part in insuring that tomorrow's world will be fairer than today's. Physicians, nurses, welfare workers, social engineers, teachers, ministers, researchers into the cause and spread of disease, wise parents, enlightened politicians, and far-visioned statesmen, these all are stalwart creators of a finer new world for men.

But it is not enough just to do all we can to bring about a more equitable social order and to relieve mankind's suffering insofar as we are able. We are called to a harder task, namely, to pour into the world all the happiness and courage we possess. We are, in other words, to make a spiritual investment in the new world. We are to pump into its veins new life, new hope, new joy. To rectify social injustice and relieve suffering is a magnificent way to use our lives. To use our strength to make a world grown tired and old a more joyous and happier place for men to dwell is even more splendid.

And since beauty that once lived never dies, men yet unborn will rejoice that we lived, if we leave behind us when our work and days are done, some beauteous thing.

Beauty in any form is the most useful thing in the world, and creators of beauty are the most useful people we know. We have forgotten the names of the engineers whose skill erected the Roman highways and aqueducts, but the creations of the artists of ancient Greece are with us still to inspire, to ennoble, and to bless. Since men do not live by bread alone but by every word and work of God, whoso builds beauty into the fabric of the world serves God and man and the future well.

Fine words, but how about the man who lacks a craftman's skill and an artist's hand? How can he aid in building beauty into the world? Our answer is ready. Though we may not leave behind us some original work of art that our skill and genius have fashioned, if we leave our fellows the memory of a beautiful life joyfully lived, we shall have performed a worthy service to those who shall follow us. Who makes the world a more beautiful place, not just by what he has done, but also by the manner and spirit in which he has lived, serves the future well. Tomorrow will surely be fairer than today because such a man was born.

Beyond all this, what further can a man do to make tomorrow better than today and to leave the world a happier place than he found it?

The Christian has an immediate answer. It is this: the best thing a man can do for the future of the world is to increase the influence of Christ within it. Here every man who regards himself in any sense of the word a Christian can take hold and help, for Christ's followers are His agents in the world, emissaries of His love and will.

It is true that every person who is engaged in any enterprise that benefits mankind mentally, morally, physically, or spiritually is helping to extend the influence of Christ. But without minimizing the value of every such endeavor, by itself it is not enough. It is not adequate for the size of the task in hand that Jesus should be remembered vaguely as the personality and power behind men's efforts to do good, to perform works of mercy and deeds of love. Men must come to know Jesus directly and this can only be brought about by men who have met Him face-to-face.

This means that men who seek to make tomorrow better than today must, first of all, be Christ's disciples themselves and as such they must, secondly, regard themselves as missionaries devoted to the winning of other men to discipleship to Him. Specifically, they must recognize that only in the following of Christ will mankind's problems be solved. Further, they must help others to share this conviction and to align their energies with Christ's purpose—the welding of the nations into one family, making God's will the dominant motive in human life, transforming the kingdoms of this world into the Kingdom of Christ.

This is simply to say that if we want to have a share in building a finer world for tomorrow, we must conceive of ourselves as co-workers with God. Working with Christ for His goals, we are working hand-in-hand with God.

Christians have always considered themselves "laborers together with God," and so do all men who judge the great use of life to be workers alongside of God assisting His plans for men to come true. There is no higher dignity that men can wear than this, no finer role in life that they can play. To use our lives, with all the strength and gifts that God has endowed them, to advance God's good purposes for mankind is a certain way to make sure that the world will be a better place for our having lived.

Winners-of-men to Christ and co-workers with God are always men of faith, and we are called to be such men if we labor for the day when earth will be "fair and all men glad and wise." Sir Robert Shirley of seventeenth-century England is the type of man we should emulate. We know little of him beyond the fact that in the year 1653, "when all things sacred were throughout the nation either demolished or profaned" by the Puritans, he established a chapel of the Church of England, the church and faith Oliver Cromwell was determined to destroy. According to the dedicatory inscription on the walls of his chapel, Sir Robert's "singular praise is to have done the best things in the worst times, and hoped them in the most calamitous."

The faith exhibited by this obscure English nobleman is the sort of faith we must possess and act by now. Faith to believe in and to perform the best things even in these perilous and unpropitious times—this is what God requires of us now, and no less than this, if we would be builders of a fairer world for men. It will be easier for us to approach the height of Sir Robert's faith and to equal his action, if we recall that countless others have done what now we are called upon to do—believe in the best things in the worst times. Wordsworth composed some of his greatest sonnets while Napoleon was preparing for the invasion of England. Keats's memorable sonnet of intellectual and spiritual discovery, "On First Looking into Chapman's Homer," was written the same summer the Battle of Waterloo was fought. Handel's majestic "Hallelujah Chorus" was written when its composer's health and fortunes were at their lowest ebb.

Those who wish to bear a hand in shaping a brave new world for men must forswear once and for all the cynicism of Alexander Pope, who, daring to add to the Beatitudes, penned the blasé line: "Blessed is he who expects nothing, for he shall never be disappointed." They will, instead, go along with William Carey, the father of Christian missions in modern times, who said, "Expect great things from God; attempt great things for God."

4. An Opportunity for Spiritual Adventure

If a man elects, as its best use, to devote his life to some goal that will outlast his own short span of years and serving which will help make the world a better place, he has chosen for himself a career of spiritual adventure. He will know raptures and sorrows hid from other men, and he will make discoveries that from other eyes are forever sealed. He will experience heartaches and suffering that he might otherwise have escaped, but he will also achieve a joy and a peace that other men do not share.

A pre-eminent use of life and one that appeals to many men as life's highest is this: an opportunity for spiritual adventure and discovery. To the adventurous and the daring, to the carefree and the young in heart, all will be revealed. Not to the timid, the hesitant, and the fearful will life disclose its secrets, share its treasures, and bestow its prizes, but only to him who can say with la Comtesse de Noailles, "Life has greatly tempted me, and as I was brave, I turned aside from neither the risk, nor the joy, nor the pain."

To regard life as a chance for spiritual adventure is one of the most exciting uses to which life can be put. To use life thus is to use it as befits a creature made in the image of God. The late Winifred Kirkland was one who chose to use her life in this manner. "I am a person who has chosen to risk her life on the reality of a spiritual adventure," she once wrote. To welcome life and to be grateful for it as an opportunity to discover day by day more about God and things divine—what could be a more perdurably exciting way to use life? To use life as a chance for spiritual adventure is to make of life a romance from first to last.

Seventy years ago Phillips Brooks, one of America's greatest preachers, wrote some words which are pertinent here:

"The great danger facing all of us—let me say it again, for one feels it tremendously—is not that we shall make an absolute failure of life, nor that we shall fall into outright viciousness, nor that we shall be terribly unhappy, nor that we shall feel life has no meaning at all—not these things. The danger is that we may fail to perceive life's greatest meaning, fall short of its highest good, miss its deepest and most abiding happiness, be unable to tender the most needed service, be unconscious of life ablaze with the light of the Presence of God—and be content to have it so—that is the danger.

"That some day we may wake up and find that always we have been busy with husks and trappings of life and have really missed life itself. For life without God, to one who has known the richness and joy of life with Him, is unthinkable, impossible. That is what one prays one's friends may be spared—satisfaction with a life that falls short of the best, that has in it no tingle or thrill which comes from a friendship with the Father."

That some day you or I may wake up and suddenly realize that for all the years past we have been occupied with the "husks and trappings of life" and in so doing have missed life itself—it is this alarming possibility which is at the root of our conviction that one of the noblest uses of life is to use it for spiritual adventure. Life is our chance to catch and enjoy what Sir Thomas Browne quaintly calls "a glimpse of Incomprehensibles, and Thoughts of things which Thoughts but tenderly touch." Life is surely too precious a gift to fritter it away in aimless, inconsequential activity or in the in-sentient existence of a clod of clay.

The man who wants to know the full richness of life, who covets knowledge of its secrets, and who would live to the utmost while he is living must accept the gift of life as an opportunity for spiritual adventure. That few men dare to live in this manner attests the fact that there really are but few who wish to know, or have the courage to discover, all that life will reveal to the inquiring student.

Yet, truly, life either is an adventure, or it is not much at all. The only way to become invulnerable in the world is, once and for all, to abandon all thoughts of safety and all yearnings for a security we were never meant to have and which at best is sure to prove stultifying. "Life must always be a great adventure, with risks on every hand; a clear-sighted eye, a many-sided sympathy, a fine daring, and end-less patience, are ever necessary to all good living," Havelock Ellis tells us. "With such qualities alone may the artist in life reach success."

There are three rungs in the ladder we must climb in order to arrive at truth: first wonder, then vision, and finally venture. The last word is the key of it all—venture. Life is a paltry and dismal affair in all honesty, if we lack a venturous heart and a daring spirit. Life must always be regarded as a great adventure with risks on every hand, and no man is safe in this world unless he swings his life between a risk and an opportunity. The best things are always to be found on the yonder side of a risk.

They are the torchbearers, we say, the people who live in response to religion's high challenge to use the gift of life as an opportunity for spiritual adventure and discovery, as a chance to enter into a knowledge of God that from timid and fearful souls is forever denied. The world would be a sorry place without them, without these few, the torchbearers, the men and women who, living midst the things of earth and time, have their hearts set wholly on things timeless and eternal, and who render life more beautiful for us all by the revelation and interpretation of the Divine their daily lives reveal. These folk, the torchbearers, bring to us a rare harvest of knowledge of the unseen and everlasting. They bring God close to us and near at hand, they help to make God vivid, they enable us to love Him more warmly, and they set our feet in pathways that lead us to His home.

How better to use one's life than in the pursuit of further knowledge of God? How better to live one's days than as an adventure of heart and mind ever seeking to discover more of God and things divine? How better to spend one's days than as a pilgrim making a journey that has as its final end and goal nothing less than the vision of God?

5. A Quest for God

The use of life as a quest for further knowledge of God stands before us. Using our lives in this manner is to embark on an adventure that will last a lifetime and beyond, but there are few more exciting options than this. To devote our lives to a seeking for the answer to Job's heart-wrung plaint, and not Job's only but every man's in every age and not least our own: "Oh that I knew where I might find him! that I might come even to his seat!"—this is a prospect of surpassing interest to him who cares more about the quality of his days than the quantity of his years.

When we pare life down to its essentials, we find there is but one thing really needful—to possess God. But how do we find and come to possess God?

Before we can expect to answer this question, however, an honest answer must be given to another upon which the success of our quest depends. The question is: Do we really want to find God? Since God is ever seeking us, like a shepherd a lost sheep, we shall surely be found by Him, unless we are evading Him and hiding from Him. The nature of God guarantees that He will find us and that we shall find Him, if such is sincerely our desire.

If after careful consideration we decide that we really want to find God and are willing to pay the price to enjoy such delight—the surrender of our cherished sins and the forswearing of our easy moral compromises, then we must face up to the ways, and there are many of them, in which we may be, right now, hiding "from the presence of the Lord God."

First, are we hiding from God in refusing to repent, in stubbornly refusing to change our way of life? Are we still determined that we ourselves, not God, shall have the right-of-way in the conduct of our lives? Are we hiding from God in refusing to yield ourselves to Him utterly, because we are afraid that He will require of us that we become more than we dare?

Second, are we hiding from God in our intellectual pretensions? We ask this, for intellectual curiosity, in itself a good thing, can easily become a spiritual foxhole in which the soul can hide from God.

It is frightfully easy, when our courage is not quite equal to making complete surrender to God's way of life, to say that intellectual doubts stand in the way. The difficulties in the way of a man who would find God, however, are seldom intellectual. More often it is some impurity, some sin, some callousness of soul, that is the blind spot. It is a lame alibi to claim that intellectual doubts obstruct progress in our quest for God when the problem is most likely, if we are fearlessly honest, a moral one.

Again, are we hiding from God in service to men? Many

men have found God through service to their fellows, but service can easily become a storm shelter in which the soul hides from God.

Service can readily become an escape from getting the first thing straight—our own personal relationship with God. We can dodge getting this matter right by keeping ourselves perpetually busy running God's errands. But the proper order is: first the Father's arms and then the Father's errands. It is first the resolution of our own moral conflicts and then service to a needy and troubled world. It is first our own sins and then our brother's need.

Then there are those folk who hide from God in misusing religion as a means of escaping from reality, when religion is, properly conceived and rightly used, the supreme way of discovering reality and dealing with it.

There is a kind of religion, especially popular in a dangerous and critical age, to which many people fly in order to escape the head-on challenges, the stern facts, and the harsh realities of life. It is one of real religion's most deadly enemies, and Christianity's in particular. Such ersatz religion is neither true religion nor does it bear any faintest resemblance to authentic Christianity. It is a subtle and devilish means of hiding from God too often adopted by people who would have us believe they have actually found Him.

Religion is neither dope nor insurance against hard blows of fortune nor is it escape from reality. If it were insurance against those harsh facts that try men's spirits, the churches would be crowded to overflowing every day. The man who has found God has not insured himself against calamity, but he has found in God power and strength to turn calamity into victory and disaster into triumph. The man who has found God will not escape the thorns of life, which come to all alike, but he will wear them as a crown.

There are other ways of hiding "from the presence of the Lord God," notably keeping oneself so feverishly busy, so constantly gyrating with activity, that one has no time to think of God. This is a most popular way of hiding from God these days, just as it is a most certain way of squeezing God out of one's life and days. Another equally popular way of hiding from God nowadays is to join the throngs who endlessly indulge themselves in the pleasures of the senses, who seek by continual and ever-new diversions not just to find "a surcease from trouble and a release from care" but to avoid coming face-to-face with reality, with God.

We have cited some of the many ways in which men can and do hide from God, all ready snares against which the seeker for God needs to be warned. Now we would suggest six steps to pursue in setting out on our quest to find God.

First, start at the furthest point we have reached. Already we have advanced further than we suspect. Enter boldly this very hour upon further search for the Father-God our fleeting vision has already in partial degree revealed.

Second, practice imaginative faith; use our imagination as the doorway into a living faith and walk by means of it into an awareness of the reality and then the love of the Father-God.

Imagination is commonly called "the eye of the soul," but imagination must be coupled with deep knowledge to be truly "the eye of the soul." Imagination is the spirit's wings; it is one of man's surest avenues of approach to God; and when it is joined with learning and wisdom, our minds penetrate into regions of perception which lie hidden from most

men's view. Imagination is not to be thought of as the faculty
by which we conjure up something that has no existence in
reality. It is the God-given faculty by which we may appre-
hend a reality, like God, the Supreme Reality, which cannot
be comprehended in any other way.

Conviction of the reality of God is never reached by ar-
gument, however cogent and compelling the metaphysics.
Knowledge of spiritual reality, unconquerable certainty of
God, living communion with the Eternal — these are
achieved through actual experience. And to have experience
we must make a venture which begins with and must be
constantly strengthened by the faculty of imagination, which
is in its own sphere as reputable and reliable as sight.

Third, we should seek to see God everywhere in His visible garment, this universe He has created. "The world is
charged with the grandeur of God," Gerald Manley Hop-
kins has rightly said.

We should never miss a chance to see anything that is
beautiful: "The soul takes wings when it sees beauty." Since
"man nor king can see unmoved the coming of a wind-
filled sail, the coming of a lovely lady, the coming of a horse
in speed," as James Stephens truly reports, we should notice
beauty everywhere—in a face, in a flower, in a storm cloud,
in the countryside in spring. Finding beauty everywhere we
discover that God signs His name all over the earth that He
has made. The seeker for God finds, as St. John of the Cross
did, that "God passes through the thicket of this world, and
wherever His glance falls He turns all things to beauty."

One of the most persuasive assurances we have of God
comes through the avenue of the beautiful. A thing of beauty is the eternal in the world about us, God alive in the pres-

ent; it is God speaking to us today. To watch the beautiful, to cherish it, and to seek for it, is to have begun to walk a pathway that leads to God.

Fourth, let us persist in the pursuit of the truth. The search for truth is bound to bring us to God, for at the end of every line of human thought the mind is confronted with God. The pursuit of truth will invariably lead us to The Truth.

Fifth, we must consecrate our imaginations to making Jesus new. It is hard for men to do this today, strangely, to win for themselves a real vision of the real Christ. Too many books and too many sermons about Him, too many stained-glass windows and too much child's talk about Him, too great familiarity with His name and too casual acquaintance with His staggering beauty, these all account for the difficulty men have today in seeking to see Him who coming from God moved among men as a white flame not so many years ago.

Yet hard as it may be to capture a real vision of the real Christ, as He was and as He is, such is our major task if we would find our way to God. When He becomes real and living before our eyes, we will find ourselves worshiping Him, and through Him, who is the truth about God, the way to God, and the life of God, presently arriving at the place where we would be.

The final suggestion is this: begin now to worship God even though our knowledge of God is far from as complete as we would have it be.

Know this for sure, that he who worships God will one day certainly find Him and be received into His fatherly embrace. Who worships God will have no need of star or angel to guide him to the Father's house. Humble love keeps the door of Heaven, and the man who worships God in sincerity and with abounding love will find God waiting to welcome him.

And, as we go forward in our quest, let us remember what Hans Denck, a seeker for God of centuries ago, said: "Apart from God no one can either seek or find God, for he who seeks God has already in truth found Him."

6. Discovering What Religion Is All About

Using our days, even while necessarily occupied with other activities, as a lifetime quest for God leads to the use of life as a personal mission to find out what religion is all about. One man says religion in its essence consists of one thing and another maintains something utterly different. One church claims religion is this, while the one next door affirms a diametrically opposite view. Small wonder people are confused and that many, in perplexity and disgust, turn away from religion, at least in its institutionalized forms, altogether! Yet every man wants to know, for religion is a vital concern of every man. It takes most men a long time, midst the conflict of competing voices, to find out the truth of the matter. Life, we believe, is well used in trying to discover the correct answer.

Each one of us has a religion, a faith, a creed, of some kind. Recognize this right at the start. Every one of us has a religion that we live by whether we realize it or not. One is forced upon us. Your religion and mine is what life has taught us and what, as we read life and interpret our experience, seems to us true and supremely worth-while and good.

When pressed for a definition of religion, many find it difficult to put into words the content of their creed, while others can do it quickly. But for every man alike his religion is that which gives unity and direction and power to his life; that which he gets excited about and concerning which he waxes eloquent and enthusiastic; that from which he derives richest sustenance for living; that which, at great personal hardship, labor and cost, he will defend and champion, struggle for, and, if need be, die. In this sense a man's religion is his master passion.

Definitions of religion abound, and perhaps agreement on just what religion is in essence will be impossible to achieve, yet it is not a waste of time to consider some of the chief ways men have understood religion. Doing this will help us if we are among those who count it a good use of life to find out for ourselves what religion is all about.

In carrying forward this task a useful procedure to follow is to examine religious experience in the light of three great approaches to spiritual reality, namely, creed, cult, and conduct. Under these three headings every religion can be described and the gist of it clearly defined for they refer to the basic elements in any religion—its intellectual structure and framework, its emotional expression, and its ethical content. Examining a religion in the light of the belief, worship, and behavior it requires suggests also Baron Friedrich von Hügel's threefold way of interpreting religion, considering it from the institutional, intellectual, and mystical aspects. And then there is William Law's view of religion as a triad of authority, reason, and experience, all three contributing to its strength and forming "a threefold cord not quickly broken."

There are but two great realities in the universe, the heart of God and the heart of man, and each is ever seeking the other. In trying to pinpoint the essence of religion, it is important to keep this fact in mind, for the religious history of mankind is simply the story of this two-way seeking and of the ways men have used in times past and use today to effect a meeting of the two. Basically, religion has to do with a joining together of God and man, so one fruitful way to view religion is as that which binds together. The very word "religion" is derived from the Latin verb *"ligare"* which means "to bind," and hence religion may be understood as that which binds together God and man, man and man, and a man within himself.

This certainly is an entirely valid way to think of religion: as that which, first of all, binds us to God, who is "the something universal" which unites all created things into a whole; as that which, second, binds us to our fellow men in a fellowship of things immortal; as that which, third, binds ourselves into a unified, integrated personality. From earliest times man has felt the tug of this threefold tie which unites him with and binds him to God, with his fellow men, and within himself, linking his solitary, little life with the vast eternal enterprise. We shall not go wrong in considering religion in this light, as that which binds things together, holds things together—heaven and earth, God and man, man and man in human society, and each man within himself as a harmonious, organic personality.

A young man born in Aberdeen, Scotland, three centuries ago and who became at the age of twenty professor of philosophy in that city's ancient university, Henry Scougal by name, offers us a second illuminating insight into the meaning of religion. Religion is not a matter of creeds and doctrines, of orthodox concepts and correct opinions, says Scougal, nor is it a matter of observing outward rites, in fulfilling prescribed duties, or in obeying certain moral taboos. "True religion," says he, "is the union of the soul with God, a real participation of the divine nature, the very image of God drawn upon the soul; or, in the Apostle's phrase, it is Christ formed within us. Briefly, I know not how the nature of religion can be more fully expressed than by calling it a Divine Life—the life of God in the soul of man." This concept of the nature of religion reminds us of the words of the Swiss savant Henri Fréderic Amiel, "To me religion is life before God and in God."

A further contribution to our quest of what religion is all about comes from one of those choice books which once discovered instantly become our dearest friends and to which we turn time and again for inspiration and comfort and command. The book is entitled *Psalms of the West* by Rolla Russell. Its sense of the divine beauty in nature, of the holiness of love, of the voice of God in reason, of the encompassing sympathy and care of the Eternal, of the strength of the ages working silently through the upheaval and tragedy of the world—all this makes it a book to live with and to love. In this book the author tells us that religion is "the love of God, the union of the spirit of man with holiness, the constant endeavor to do the best and beat the worst." We cherish Rolla Russell's definition of the essence of religion, words which remind us of Ralph Waldo Emerson's statement that religion, or, as he calls it, the secret of life, is "the doing of all good, and for its sake the suffering of all evil."

The dying hours of Henry David Thoreau afford us another insight. As Thoreau lay dying, a dear old aunt be-
sought him to make his peace with God. He replied, "But
I have never quarreled with God." Later, in response to a
more insistent plea that he prepare for life in the world
beyond death, he said, "One world at a time."

"One world at a time" commends itself as a thoroughly
sensible course, and so it would be if only it were possible.
But man is an amphibious being, a citizen of two worlds,
and he is built to dwell in both worlds at one and the same
time. Further, these two worlds are so interwoven that man
cannot, even if he would, live in one to the exclusion of the
other without ceasing to be fully a man. Religion is this
recognition of the two worlds which are man's home and
man's endeavor to live in both at one and the same time,
this world of the here and now and the eternal world whence
we came and to which on death we return.

Turning to the Holy Bible we find in its pages many eloquent definitions of religion. Perhaps the most memorable
of all is that of Micah who speaks for all the wise and holy
men of Israel when he says: "He hath showed thee, O man,
what is good; and what doth the Lord require of thee, but
to do justly, and to love mercy, and to walk humbly with
thy God?" (Micah 6:8). This text should be carved upon
every shrine of worship, if only to remind us that religion,
in its basic motivation and truest manifestation, is not a sys-
tem nor a creed nor a ritual, but a quiet, humble, honest
way of living before God and man a life of righteousness
and justice, of mercy and love.

What has Christianity to say? How does it understand and
define religion?

We shall have the answer to these questions when we recall that Christianity is primarily a message from God and about God and that it is the faith and way of living that result when a man hears that message and responds to it, accepting it as truth. It is first and foremost a revelation of the nature of God as proved in what God has done. A revelation before it is a religion, Christianity is born in a man when he accepts the good news the Church for nineteen centuries has proclaimed, namely, that God out of His mercy and on His own initiative, has acted for man's deliverance from the tyranny of evil and sin and death; that God out of His love has made a way to man who by searching and seeking could not otherwise get to Him; that God has not left man alone but cares for every man with a love surpassing human understanding. Christianity is the faith that issues from hearing and believing this good news of God Himself coming to earth in His Son Jesus Christ to set men free, to restore them to Himself, to give them eternal life, and to draw them all within the reach of His saving embrace.

Jesus of Nazareth, who Himself was the good news that the religion which bears His name heralds to all mankind, never once used the word "religion." The word He always used instead was "Life." He came, He said, that men might have life and that they might have it more abundantly. Real life, the kind of life God Himself enjoys, the quality of life He called "eternal life"—this is what Jesus came bringing to men. If men accept God's gift to them in Christ, then the religion of Christ becomes, in the words of Adolf Harnack, "eternal life in the midst of time, by the strength and under the eyes of God."

Going on to a study of the Gospel records and mulling over in our minds what, according to them, the word "religion" signified to Jesus in His days on earth, it becomes clear that it meant three things mainly: following in Jesus' steps, trusting in God and obeying His will, and resting in the Lord. This, I believe, is the heart of Christianity for everyday people living their everyday lives.

What is religion all about? A lifetime can be consumed in discovering the answer, for innumerably more views than we have listed come readily to mind. For one, there is Albert Schweitzer's noble concept of religion as being essentially "reverence for life," for all living things. There is Brother Lawrence's thought of religion as living continually in the presence of God. Then we think of Thomas à Kempis' *Imitation of Christ* and Lucretius' "beholding all with a peaceful soul."

No life is idly wasted or foolishly spent in finding out what religion is all about. We have here suggested only a few of the many and varying interpretations wise and holy men have suggested and lived by through the years. But however we define religion and understand it, we come to see eventually that it is a matter of a vertical and a horizontal orientation, the while it has its center in one's self. It must have an upward thrust, linking our transitory and tormented lives with the timeless, eternal life of God. Then there must be an outward movement, because of our affiliation with God and our sharing in His mercy and love, which impels us to serve our brothers in their need. And all the while there must be at the heart integrity and purity in one's own life. Filial faith—a child's trust in his father; human compassion —not just pity for, but suffering with, our fellows; inward purity in our own lives—these are the essential elements in true religion.

Beyond these the profoundest thinker cannot go and short of them the simplest believer must not stop. Reverence and Adoration, Sympathy and Service, Personal Holiness and Heroic Virtue—these words sum up what religion is all about, and to this list a further and inescapable note must be added—gratitude to God for His being, for His being what He is, and for His doing what He has done in Christ to effect our redemption and to secure for us our salvation. To adoration and compassion, to holiness and gratitude to God, high religion calls us as our highest duty and as our chief glory as men created in the image of God.

7. *The Worship of God*

Those who act upon the conviction that the highest use of life is its opportunity for spiritual adventure and a quest for God need no further persuasion to believe that one of its chief employments lies in the service and worship of God. The majesty and holiness, the beauty and love, their eyes have seen—these bend them to adoration and worship and praise. To use life for the worship of Almighty God seems to such people inevitable, entirely normal and natural, and just what life was given them to do. To such people life has no use surpassing in importance the worship of God, the praise of His Holy Name, and the enjoyment of Him while on earth and beyond death in heaven.

However, if we judge by the evidence of the country's none too crowded churches, the worship of God is for millions today no such sheer delight and certainly not one of the principal uses of life. Even for those who do pause in the frenzied whirl to acknowledge the sovereignty of God, the act of worship is apt to be more a duty than a privilege and not the spontaneous action of a soul in love with God. And, as everyone is vividly aware, freedom of worship has become for millions in our time freedom not to worship at all.

Now this is a matter for grave alarm, since the history of the Christian Church indicates that the temper and tone of its worship is an accurate index to its spiritual temperature. Today in countless churches throughout the land the worship of God is a humdrum and pedestrian business, unimaginative and mechanical, a routine occupation lacking vibrancy and exaltation and quite devoid of joy and passion and zeal. One wonders if the Church is half dead or dying and if it no longer believes its own good news about God!

Clearly, the art of worship must be relearned, or perhaps learned for the first time, by today's generation of churchmen, else the witness to God among men will be far from radiant and compelling in the years ahead. Worship is so much more than what today's sorry caricatures would lead a man to believe. It is so much more than "going to church," wearily singing a few sentimental hymns, patiently kneeling while the minister reads or says the prayers, and restlessly sitting through a sermon which is liable to be uninspired and uninspiring.

But what is worship? you ask, you who would honor and praise the majesty and holiness, the beauty and love, you call by the name of God.

First of all, worship is the acknowledgment of the supreme worth-ship of God. That is what the word means—the worth-ship of God. Men are prone to place things first in order of importance, man second, and God last, whereas the proper order is God first, man second, and things last. God is first and foremost and above all else—this is the significance of worshiping God. Worship is just the declaring that of all persons and things in heaven and on earth God is the supremely most worth-while. To the religious man worship is natural and automatic, for to him God is the highest good, that which is most deserving of service and praise, but to the man who does not worship, God is patently not important at all. His life, he plainly believes, is full and complete without God. Using any of his time for the worship of God is definitely not for him.

Second, worship is an experience, and when we worship "in spirit and in truth" something happens to us and in us and through us. Though worship must inevitably express itself in form and in some regularized order, it is not primarily a form; it is, above all, an experience. "At its best and truest," Rufus M. Jones has said, "worship seems to me to be the direct, vital, joyous, personal experience and practice of the presence of God."

Third, worship is the adoration of God, of His Being and Beauty. More even than "the manifestation of reverence in the presence of God," worship is pre-eminently the adoration of God, "the pouring out of our soul to God in sheer adoration of His greatness and gratitude for His goodness." Adoration and heroic virtue are the sum of religion according to Baron von Hügel.

To many men worship is awed wonder in the presence of God. This is as good a place as any to begin, for from hushed wonder before God we move easily to adoration. Our first wonder may spring from ignorance, but our last wonder will flow from admiration and will lead to adoration.

The late Archbishop of Canterbury's definition sums up the essence of worship as well as any short statement we know. "To worship," wrote Dr. William Temple, "is to quicken the conscience by the holiness of God, to feed the mind with the truth of God, to purge the imagination by the beauty of God, to open the heart to the love of God, to devote the will to the purpose of God. All this gathered up in that emotion which most cleanses us from selfishness because it is the most selfless of all emotions—adoration."

To the Christian, worship is all these things and one thing more: it is a giving to God. It is a giving to God the honor and homage properly due His Name; and then it is a giving to God of oneself, with nothing held back. It is an offering of one's life, one's love, one's all, for no less than this does God desire or deserve.

If we seek to know what worship is for the Christian, in the service of the Holy Communion we may see and know. Called by whatever name one prefers, the Liturgy of the Church is the central act of worship for Christian men. Here is Christian worship at its highest, at its truest, and at its best. In this sacrament is revealed the heart of Christian life, belief, and devotion; and though it is, no matter how elaborately or how plainly celebrated, a wondrously simple rite, it is marvelously bigger and greater than we. Its treasure is never exhausted, and it fills every man's deepest religious need. The Lord's own service, it is a symbol of that total self-offering, of that complete self-giving, that is the Christian disciple's highest privilege to make to God as his paramount act of worship.

"This our sacrifice of praise and thanksgiving"—we like to think of the Holy Communion in this light. It is our sacrifice of praise to God, gladly rendered, simply for His being and for His being what He is. And then it is our sacrifice of thanksgiving to God for His doing what He has done and for what He continues to do. It is particularly an articulation of our gratitude for God's greatest gift, His Son, and for His Son's birth, life, death, and resurrection in triumph over men's final foe, the grave. To use the theologians' words, it is a corporate act of thanksgiving for the Incarnation, the Atonement, and the Resurrection, or for Forgiveness, Redemption, and Salvation.

This, the Lord's own service, is the Christian's sacrifice of thanksgiving and praise; and, when we join in its celebration, we know that here we are doing what the Lord of Life Himself commanded us to do, and further that here we are engaging in distinctly Christian worship at its highest, and that here God comes silently to us if in faith and expectancy we draw near to Him.

8. Increase in Reverence and Love toward God

Those who use their lives for the worship and praise of God presently find themselves not only growing in knowledge of God, but also steadily increasing in reverence and love toward Him. The more they learn of God, the more profound their reverence becomes and the higher their love for God mounts. This should not be surprising, for one of the purposes life serves is, because of what we see and learn and discover, to grow in reverence and love toward the Creator-Father God of the universe.

On Mr. Gladstone's last visit to Oxford, he is reported to have sat in the senior common room of Christ Church College and discoursed at length upon the happy changes he had witnessed during his lifetime in the lot of the English people. His outlook was so radiantly optimistic that it aroused a challenge.

"Are we to understand, sir," asked one student, "that you have no anxieties for the future? Are there no adverse signs?"

The old statesman answered slowly: "Yes, there is one thing which frightens me. The fear of God seems to be dying out in the minds of men."

What frightened the "grand old man" of England more than fifty years ago is a prospect even more alarming today. That fear of God which is the beginning point of all real religion means little or nothing to millions of people nowadays. Of fear we know too much: it is the modern demon. But of the fear of God we know far too little. Yet one of the great uses of life is to grow in reverence for God and to increase in love for His most Holy Name.

Fear of God is the starting point of knowledge as well as of all real religion. No man has ever penetrated far and deep into the secrets and the mysteries of God's created universe who was not first a man who walked in awe of the Timeless and the Eternal. Robert Boyle, for example, was such a man. A seventeenth-century scientist, he never mentioned the name of God without a visible and reverent pause. Awed reverence for God precedes coming into knowledge of His Being and ways.

Fear of God, that deep reverence for the Almighty Creator which pervades the whole Old Testament, is the chief power and joy of life. "The true joy of man is in doing that which is most proper to his nature," declared Marcus Aurelius. "That which is most proper to his nature," according to Ignatius, the martyr bishop of Antioch, is "to praise, to reverence, and to serve God our Lord."

All religious men believe this. Oliver Wendell Holmes once remarked: "I have in my breast a plant called reverence. I go to church to have it watered." Katherine Mansfield, another figure of literary fame, also knew wherein lay "the true joy of man." One day a visitor paid extravagant praise to her poems. "There is not one of them," she replied in a soft voice, "that I could show to God."

Again, reverence for God and for God alone enables a man to walk through life a free man unafraid. The man who fears God alone is free. He is liberated from all other fears. Of God alone should we be afraid, and our only care, our only fear, should be not to offend His love and disobey His will. Cardinal Mercier once remarked, "The greater the fear of God, the less the fear of man." True, and the greater our fear of God, the less will be our fear of anything life can or may do to us.

Reverence for God is the soul of religion, as fellowship with God in prayer is its heart. Ever has it been so. Primitive man lived in dread and terror of God, the power which caused flood and avalanche, fire and famine, earthquake and storm. Men of all the Bible centuries and of ancient Greece and Rome lived in reverent respect of God, as did men in all the great ages of faith. Modern man, however, has in large measure forfeited that fear of God and that reverence for God which have always marked the religious man. Nevertheless, it still holds true that there is no real religion where there is but scant reverence for God in the heart. Religion begins in reverence for God, it lives by love toward God, and it reaches its climax and fulfillment in the adoration of God.

Without reverence for the Eternal the quest for God is a futile errand. Without reverence and love toward God religion can never become vital and vibrant and find an abiding place in the heart of a man. Unless we are growing day by day in reverence and love toward God, the Author, Preserver, and Finisher of Creation, we shall never know God as we yearn to know Him and as the child and the saint actually do.

Until we have love for God, men wise in spiritual things believe, it is well that we should have fear. But if we have fear, we will presently have love. And life has no finer use than this, to increase in reverence and love toward God the Father Almighty.

9. Friendship with God

Viewed as an adventure of heart and mind, of spirit and will, in pursuit of ever-widening knowledge of God and things divine, life takes on the color and flavor of romance. Each morning arrives with the promise of fresh discoveries to be made, new heights of spiritual experience to be climbed. Worship leads to increased reverence toward God and greater love for God, and day by day friendship with God deepens until it becomes a glowing reality investing every day with fragrance and power.

To use his days to become a friend of God is one of the chief uses of life to the man who believes that he has come from God and to God one day will return. Such a man holds that the time he is granted on earth is most advantageously used in establishing a firm and happy relationship with Him in whose presence he expects to dwell through all eternity.

But how do we become a friend of God? The first step is obvious, namely, by quiet, religious living and faithful worship of God. The end product of years of humbly walking with God is the friendship of God and, even more than that, union with the Divine.

The second step in becoming a friend of God is to use our loneliness as an avenue to God. By way of the religious use of loneliness many a man has found his way to God and to the comfort of His friendship and love.

All too many are the enemies of happiness, but of them all loneliness stands alone and apart as the greatest sorrow of mankind. Every man is required in life to learn how to deal with solitude, how to make of it not a foe but a friend, or fall a casualty in living.

Loneliness is one of the given conditions of life. We enter life alone and we depart alone, and in this world we live as we dream—alone. In all the chief matters of life we are alone, and the true history of any soul is seldom deciphered by another. Often barren and appalling, loneliness is considered by many men an unmitigated curse, but if it is such, it is an affliction common to all mankind. If it is man's most grievous sorrow, it is a sorrow every man born into the world is called upon to bear. To be conscious of our aloneness in the world and to be acutely aware of our solitariness among men is simply to be sharing in the experience of every man.

There are two things we can do with our loneliness. We can run away from it or we can learn to live with it and utilize it for our soul's happiness and growth. The first alternative is ruled out, for in vain shall we seek to evade its grip. By ourselves or in a crowd we are alone. Essentially each man lives solitary and alone. Since we cannot escape loneliness, our only recourse is to use it for our soul's profit. By this we mean to transform our loneliness into solitude and to learn through loneliness shared with God the joys of companionship with One who is nearer to us than breathing and closer than hands or feet.

Alfred North Whitehead once wrote that religion is what a man does with his solitariness. This is not, of course, the whole story about religion, but a valid insight lies in his words. A man's religion is in a very real sense the adjustment he has made to the hard fact of his essential and inevitable loneliness. A man's religion is a secret affair, a private bond between himself and God, a unique relationship that alone and in aloneness he has established with his maker and the guide of his destiny. It is something that is born out of an acute awareness of one's solitariness, that is nurtured in loneliness shared with God, and that is made strong and tall by walking bravely through the world alone with God.

Loneliness can be a blessing or a curse. To some men it is a veritable demon. It drives them to alcoholism, into all kinds of foolish and sinful and desperate actions, even to suicide. Yet to other men it is the way through to God, the means by which they have come into a relationship with the Divine that is for them their true religion. It is in their loneliness that many men have discovered God and felt their way through cold emptiness and black silence to the time and day when, joyfully, they found their hands firmly held by the Father's tender grasp.

Yes, our loneliness can be either our undoing, literally, or the avenue by which we arrive at the destination where we would be—the friendship of the Heavenly Father. It can, if we let it, drive us to drink, into horrible sin, into insanity, into blind despair. But also, let us not forget, there is nothing in the world to prevent us from opening our solitude to God and sharing our aloneness with Him. Loneliness so used is a most sure way of entering into intimate companionship with God.

Living closely with God in prayer is the means by which most men become friends with God and friends of God.

The man who aspires to friendship with God finds out right at the start that prayer is no esoteric art reserved for the spiritually élite or for those already well advanced in the skills of the spiritual life. He discovers that it is the normal and natural and entirely unself-conscious way whereby he comes to know God as his constant companion and friend of friends. For such a man, prayer is not a formal religious act that he does only in church or at his bedside, a ritualized performance carried out in a prescribed manner and time and place. It is, for such a man, simply a walking with God from dawn to dark, just living continually in God's presence. It is living with his whole being alive to God, opened-up to God, oriented toward God, and geared to heeding and obeying God's will.

So understood, prayer becomes in due order a continual conversation with God, an intercourse, a communion, a way of living, which brings forth gifts of the spirit all men seek—tranquillity of mind and stability of soul, unshatterable peace and abiding power, cheer for living and good courage even for dying. Above all, such prayer makes for friendship between God and man. The most elemental definition of prayer, and also the most profound, is that of loving, trustful intercourse between friend and friend, between child and father, between creature and creator. By living with God on this basis friendship with God is won and maintained and the goal which is the aim of all prayer, union with God, is ultimately obtained.

A further way of becoming a friend of God is to have a secret garden of the soul, private and all one's own, in which a man as a seeker for God may enjoy communion with his heart's desire.

It is imperative in these tense and trying times to have a place of retirement, a sanctuary and place of retreat, ever at hand for fellowship with God, for renewal and refreshment, and for peace. Such a private haven and refuge is a prior need these days, if we would maintain serene quiet within, have a spiritual life so firm and secure that nothing can overthrow it, and enjoy what we esteem life's greatest privilege and rarest prize—friendship with God. We must find or make within the framework of our days space for companionship with God.

There are some people who will want to enter such a garden too often and linger in it too long. This is a temptation peace-loving souls must combat, for the garden's refreshing solitude can easily become an enervating narcotic. It is all too easy to use the garden as a place of escape from the wearing pressures and struggles, the burning questions and searching issues, which harass the soul in the turmoil and heat of everyday living.

While there is this danger, a more immediate one is not having and using such a quiet place to meet with God. To walk with God in the garden in the cool of day seems to many people a misuse or a waste of time when there is so much to be done. Indeed, for most people nowadays there is no cool of day—it is always sweltering high noon. With all we have to do, or think we have to do, there just seems to be no time to attend to the soul's nurture and growth.

But he who is seriously interested in becoming a friend of God knows well the value of hours spent in communion with God in the secret garden of the soul. He is everlastingly grateful for the blessings that have accrued to him by such withdrawal from the clangor and strain of the world to draw close to the Source of Life and Love and Power and Grace. The chief of all these blessings is coming to know God as a child knows a loving father and as a friend who by walking intimately with his friend enters into knowledge of the secrets of his heart. Good words to remember are those inscribed on a wall plaque in an old English garden:

> Men go to their garden for pleasure;
>   Go, thou, to thy garden for prayer;
> The Lord walks in the cool of the evening
>   With those who seek sanctuary there.

We achieve friendship with God by worshiping Him, by sharing our heart's loneliness with Him, by drawing close to Him in prayer, and by companying with Him in the secret garden of the soul. But two more things must be said. The first is this: if we covet friendship with God and seek the comfort of His love, we must be obedient servants of His will. We must school ourselves to heed His commands. The reward of obedience to God's will is friendship with God: only His faithful servants know the wonder and the beauty of His love.

Finally, if we would be friends of God, we must live in friendship with His Son. The friend of Jesus is the person who will know the joys of friendship with God, for it is through the gateway of our friendship with the Son that we enter into warm friendship with the Father. No man who does not love the Christ and follow in His steps will ever enjoy the friendship of God who out of His love sent the Christ to men.

If we seek the friendship of God, a blessing which no other in life can equal, we must first and finally love God's Son, and we must gladly and freely offer our lives to Him in loving allegiance and devoted love. If we want God's friendship for our own, we must love His Son more than friends or family or any of the things men commonly count good in life. If we want God to be our friend and if we aspire to be friends of God, we must humbly love and courageously follow God's Son to the end of our days, always remembering that through God's will, loved and done, lies the one sure pathway to His love.

10. Grow in Trust and Faith in God

Whoever counts his days well employed in becoming a friend of God also regards life as the framework for learning the fundamental lesson the years seem designed to teach—trust and faith in God.

There comes to every man as he moves through his days more than enough trouble. There are few men who do not think they are called upon to bear just about as much hard luck and adversity as a man should rightfully be afflicted with. Self-pity, that most loathsome of all vices, is easy to fall into, unless a man is constantly on his guard and firmly resolved to use life as a golden chance to grow in trust and faith in God, in God whose ways and works are often so bewilderingly difficult to understand.

Life is undeniably a strange affair and a mystifying business. How life works out, how life goes, is in all truth a baffling and curious thing. And there's no point and little sense in getting resentful at the universe because things do not work out according to our pleasure and will, for the universe will not be influenced one iota by our wrath or by our railings. If anything, it will only be amused. Frankly and bluntly, life requires us to be men of faith and trust in God, lest we succumb to cynicism and pessimism and despair.

In this situation as in every other it is best to face the fact: life is a strange and mysterious business, the way it works out, the way it goes. But human life has no monopoly on the mysterious and perplexing. Science is full of awesome mysteries and religion is too, though, judging by the way people commonly talk, we might think that only religion is beset with the element of mystery while everything in the realm of science is perfectly clear and rationally demonstrable. The fact of the matter is that present-day science reels with staggering mysteries. The Christian doctrine of the Holy Trinity makes light reading in comparison with our day's nuclear physics. What the high festivals of the Christian Year commemorate and celebrate is easier for many men to understand than the intricacies of modern electronic research. Why a tulip has a heat of $4\frac{1}{2}$ degrees above the atmosphere, why the song of a lark is always pitched precisely in the same key, why bees make their combs hexagonal—these matters are as hard for many men to comprehend as why and how God became a man and died for men. And, if the realm of religion and the external world are full of mysteries, the world within each one of us, we are told, is a region of even vaster mystery and wonder. Indeed all life, it would seem, is full of mystery, and one is not surprised that George Santayana sees the universe smiling at the frantic efforts we comic little creatures called men expend in trying to solve its riddles.

The bald, simple fact stands before us: all life is replete

with mystery and with the hard to understand. There is so much we cannot figure out and apparently are not meant to comprehend! There is so much we have to take on faith, so much we are compelled to accept in quiet trust, that it strikes us that life is designed to be, in one sense, just a long and unending discipline in perfecting ourselves in faith in the wisdom of God and in trust in His care and love. The highest pinnacle of the spiritual life, we know, is not unceasing joy in unbroken celestial sunshine, but winning through in this life to absolute trust in the love of God for ourselves and all men. Life is well used, we believe, and perhaps no better used, in seeking through our days to arrive at this point.

The fact that life is such a mysterious affair and living such a mystifying experience really should be no cause for dismay. There are definite advantages in having it this way. The first is that the mystery element in life makes human life possible. We have to be kept "in the dark" concerning the future, we need the limitations of sight, perception, and emotional response placed upon us, if we are to live not only well but at all today.

If you or I knew right now all that is in store for us in the years to come, what we will be called upon to suffer and to endure before life is over and when and where and how we are going to die, we would be paralyzed by the prospect. Be glad, we say, not angry, because we are kept "in the dark" regarding what lies ahead.

Be glad, too, for the limitations of perception and emotional response under which we live. It is a wonderful and a marvelous thing to be electrically alive, and it is tragic that so few people are, but it is a dangerous thing too. If any of us were acutely sensitive to all the misery and anguish in the world this moment, and intimate sharers of it, we would perish: our hearts would explode under the pressure. Likewise, if any of us knew, tasted, or shared all the joy in the world at any one moment, we would die of the ecstasy.

We put blinders on horses to keep their eyes focused straight ahead, to keep them in the road, and thus they pull their loads better. God, it would seem, puts blinders on our eyes that our sight will be directed straight ahead—the direction in which life moves—in order that we may pull our loads better, yes, but also that we may live happily, creatively, and serenely today.

The factor of mystery in life, the element of surprise, and the fact that our knowledge is perforce limited, all conspire to make life interesting. This is the second benefit of living in our mysterious universe and being required to live our days with a question mark always before us.

Life is monotonous and drab and dull for most people. Each day is but a weary repetition of yesterday and tomorrow can hardly be expected to offer any exciting variation. But for the man who is alive and wants to keep on being so, the mystery of life, of what is coming next, of what might possibly happen tomorrow, prevents life from becoming a boresome routine. Uncertainty and danger and the chance that something wonderful and different from the prosaic pattern of today might happen tomorrow are a big part of what makes life an exciting adventure worth the living.

The mystery of it all, of life and living, not only makes existence tolerable and possible and interesting. It serves a higher and finer purpose: it serves to bend us to humility, to create in us a sense of dependence on God, and to develop in us an attitude of faith in God and trust in His love. These three qualities—reverence, humility, and trustfulness—are the keystone in the arch of religious living; and, as we read it, life seems to be so arranged that these attitudes of heart and mind and spirit are developed in us. It is our ignorance, our sense of encompassing mystery, and our wonderment in the face of how life unfolds, that make us reverent and humble and trustful. It is these very things that make us feel around in the dark for the Father's hand and keep us groping hopefully until we find it.

Yes, life has its mysteries and so also do science and religion, but religion's are mysteries not of darkness but of light. We are as children setting out across the wide and terrifying reaches of eternity on our pilgrimage to our fatherland, the home and presence of God. Religion comes to us as we begin our progress and whispers to us of the trail to follow. It is called "The Way." It starts at the font of Baptism where we join the company of a mighty army traversing the same route to God. As we walk along, the path soon becomes a broad highway worn smooth by millions of pilgrim feet which have trod the same course before. Ever and again side paths lure us off the road and we find ourselves lost and have to beat our way back to the highway again. But there is always a way back, and a welcome when we return, and brother travelers in whose fellowship we can share. And, while "The Way" is continually marked by new discoveries, insights, and horizons suddenly come into view, the one great luminous mystery of all, as we march along, is "a sense of divine companionship, of guidance, of

leading, of protection, a feeling of strong hands that have
been wounded and have come back to hold our hands, a
consciousness of feet that passed this way long years ago
and have returned to guide and stay our wayward, falter-
ing feet." Fortified by pilgrim companions and strengthened
by the divine presence, we march on through life and
through the gateway of death unto our final home, the
vision of God.

So far as the element of mystery in life is concerned, the
man of religion is a man of faith and trust in Him who is
the author and finisher of his faith. Though he is often
puzzled and staggered by the way life goes, he knows God
writes straight though with crooked lines, and he says hon-
estly and sincerely:

> I would rather walk in the dark with God
>   Than go alone in the light;
> I would rather walk with Him by faith
>   Than walk alone by sight.[1]

[1] Mary Gardner Brainard, "Faith and Sight."

11. The Service of God

He who regards life as an opportunity for high spiritual adventure counts as one of its foremost uses the service of God. His desire is to be more than just a seeker for God and a worshiper of His holy Name. He wants to be more than a learner of God, even more than a friend of God. His aspiration is to be a servant of the Most High.

Just what does it mean to give one's life, to employ one's life, in the service of God?

We can answer that question by enumerating several of the things a man must expect who chooses God as his master and the Kingdom of God as the object of his steadfast devotion.

Choosing God as the master to be served will mean not living by the time clock. The servant of God knows no end or limit to his labors. He does not work on a forty-hour basis with extra pay for overtime, but in this respect he is to be envied, not pitied. He is fortunate to be engaged in activity he enjoys with all of his being. He is not trapped in some monotonous job he endures only for the money it pays.

Using life in the service of God means living one's days in the light of a vision which once seen one can never forget, the vision of God's love and will regnant in the lives of men. And this is no easy task, for in the heat and dust, the stress and strain, of the daily round, the vision is apt to fade, grow dim, even vanish utterly. But this, no less, is the challenge of the task the servant of God has taken upon himself: midst the fever of life to keep it before his eyes, to enlarge it, and not to let it escape his grasp.

The use of life, moreover, viewed as serving God as one's master involves waging a constant warfare against sin, the world, and the devil, all three of them intensely real and active enemies of the Christian disciple. Perpetual struggle against the enemies of the Christian life and of God's Kingdom—this is the assignment of the servant of God.

High courage is called for here. Men willing to be heroes and men willing to risk becoming saints, only such need apply for duty in the ranks of those who propose to offer their lives in the service of God. And one does not have to leave his home to be a hero for Christ and a soldier of God. There is often more sterling loyalty and gallant heroism in some humble house in any ordinary street than in some romantic faraway place or spectacular vocation. Wherever it is we are appointed to serve God and in whatever capacity our loyalty and love are to be shown, there is a man's work to be done; yea, work for more than a man if one would be a faithful servant of the Most High.

Further, using life in and for the service of God involves the duty of loving as high as God and as wide as humanity. And say not, thoughtlessly, that this is a small thing, for nothing is harder to do than love all the time, be God the object of our affection, or our fellow men, or our partner in marriage. Our hearts are just not strong enough to love every moment, yet the service of God means this fearsome duty is ours, this mighty obligation to love and to love all the time in spite of everything.

Finally, there is suffering to be endured. He who would use his days in the service of God should know this at the outset. This is the cost of allegiance to God: a weight of suffering to be borne. It is no holiday outing, resolving to use one's life in the service of God and in the upbuilding of the Divine Kingdom. There will be heavy burdens to be carried and stern hardships and grievous suffering to be endured, but without pain there is no glory. He who would serve God, let him sit down and reckon with the cost, so that when hard-going comes upon him he will not be surprised or overborne. The badge of the servant of God is a cross, and who chooses to serve God will certainly be called upon to discover in his own experience the meaning of Christ's self-offering in love on Golgotha.

All this is included in using one's life in the service of God and of things divine, but there is also abundant reward. Serving God in high place or low is a perdurable joy and the satisfactions far exceed any sacrifice entailed. And lest any man think he is being superlatively noble in spending his life in the service of God, let him remember that there really is no special heroism in following the apostolic vocation. It is choosing to live a life which guarantees a man happiness and rewards he can find in no other way. It is to live the way all men recognize as the most worthwhile. It is to live a life that is empowered by a splendid purpose, one which never fails to inspire and to keep enthusiasm and aspiration alive. It is to live a life of courageous freedom, of security in peril, of abundance in the midst of want, of peace in the midst of care, and of large fellowship in the heart's loneliness. Above all, it is to live after the pattern of Christ in this world, to walk in the pathways His feet have trod, to die His death, and to rise with Him into everlasting life.

12. To Get Ready
for Your Cross

The person who proposes to devote his or her life to the service of God in this world is well advised to make use of the days at hand as preparation for the crucifixion that is sure to come. Honesty and a respect for reality compel us to urge this use of life, for a cross, a crucifixion, in a literal or figurative sense, is bound to come to the person who makes this venture.

We can escape crucifixion. Jesus could have escaped His. But if He had not accepted it, men would not today acknowledge Him as Christians do, as the Christ. He would be honored and admired, but He would not be worshiped. Of course, it is possible to avoid what no man, even the Son of God, willingly seeks and gladly embraces, but it is not possible for us to escape a cross any more than it was for Jesus if we intend to be God's servants in any comparable degree to His devotion. Because this is so, we press upon him who elects to spend his days as a servant of God using them to get ready for the crucifixion that is sure to come.

No Christian life and for that matter no life of highest aspiration can or will avoid Calvary, for whenever we choose something high, we choose a cross. We court pain when we woo an ideal and we ensure for ourselves a cross if we pursue it faithfully. And if we essay to live a Christian life to our uttermost capacity, we find it hard to believe that we shall escape a cross. Jesus lived the sample Christian life and the whole story of Holy Week climaxing in His Crucifixion tells us what we may expect if we propose to walk in His steps. It is difficult to see how our destiny can be essentially different from His, if we are men dedicated to the performance of the heavenly Father's will.

It should not shock us to be told that a crucifixion stands in front of us before we end our earthly pilgrimage, for a cross is a standard element in any and every specifically Christian life. No Christian life, we say it again, can or will avoid Calvary, though we come to Calvary, each one of us, by different routes. Use life, therefore, if you are one who is brave enough to live it as a servant of God and as a disciple of Christ, to get ready for your cross when it comes, for come it surely will.

A cross, no less, awaits the person who seeks to serve God's will in this life, for a cross is the price that must be paid for not conforming to this world's code. Calvary tells us a truth we forget to our soul's peril, that we must conform or be crucified. If we dare to be different, if we dare to use our lives in a way that varies from the pattern of men whose interest is centered only on this world, we will have to pay the price, a cross. Conformity to this world's standards is the price demanded for a safe passage through this life. Crucifixion is the destiny of the man who makes bold to live his life as a faithful servant of God's will.

There were three crosses on that hill outside Jerusalem's walls that day Christendom cannot forget. One was for a man who was too good and two were for men who were too bad. All three men who were nailed to those crosses that day were nonconformists and quite naturally they were crucified. It was inevitable. The thieves were too bad for this world and Jesus was far too good, so the world was getting them out of the way.

The prospect of a cross in store for him should not cause the servant of God to stagger and reel with shock and fear, for such a man surely knows that the world is built up, if built up at all, on the lives of broken men. It would seem that to further an ideal a man must be crucified for it. It would seem that the willingness to be broken for a cause, to die if need be for an ideal, is the true gauge of a man's devotion to the ideal he professes to serve.

Regarding the cross that one day is bound to come to the person who dares to live his or her days as a servant of the will of the Most High, let us remember several truths. The first is given to us by the sage and saintly Curé d'Ars: "Our greatest cross is the fear of crosses."

These oh so true words remind us that the way to prepare for shouldering a cross is not to live in dread of it. So doing will only reduce our capacity to bear it, will only weaken our ability to carry it. To fear our cross is only to make it the harder to carry, and to repel it when it comes is only to make it all the heavier to bear. Therefore, in Samuel Rutherford's solemnly beautiful and quaint way of saying it, "Take kindly and heartsomely with the cross, who never yet slew a child with the cross."

To bear our cross with gallant patience is the sure sign that we are Christ's disciples and like Him truly servants of the Most High. We only follow "the pioneer of life," to use Moffatt's phrase, when we bear, each man of us, our own cross with the same fortitude as He endured His. To shrink from our cross is to show all the world we are not His disciples. We are His disciples only insofar as we share in our own lives His suffering and rejection and death. We can rightfully claim His name as ours only when we endure the suffering which is the fruit of an exclusive allegiance to Him, the suffering which is an essential part of the specifically Christian life. "The cross is laid on every Christian," Dietrich Bonhoeffer reminds us, and to wriggle out from it is to deny Him who made it the symbol of discipleship in His name.

Another thing: if every call to Christ and His righteousness is a call to suffering, it is equally true that every call to suffering is a call to Christ, a promotion, an invitation to come up higher. There is strong comfort in this truth.

And let us not forget that after Good Friday came Easter Day, that following Crucifixion came Resurrection. If we endure our Good Friday, we shall then know the joys of Easter Day. Easter Day completes Good Friday and resurrection into glory is our final reward if we suffer a cross. The Cross was not the end for Jesus, but rather the beginning; and so it will be for us. But the Cross had to be suffered before all that followed after could come to pass. We come to Easter by way of Good Friday and only by traveling that route: no crucifixion, no resurrection; no suffering, no glory.

When our cross comes, let us then remember and follow

Lorenzo Scupoli's rule: "Every morning receive thine own special cross from the hands of thy Heavenly Father." Yes, let us do this, for taking up our cross is no heroic action done once and for all. It consists in the daily denying of ourselves, the daily dying with Christ all over again, the taking up our cross each day anew, and valiantly following Him who won life eternal for all men by dying for all mankind.

If we would serve God, if we would be Christ's disciples, then let us not live in fear of the cross which is the emblem of the servant of God's will and love or in dread of it. When our turn comes to walk The Way of Sorrow because of our obedience, God will grant us full grace to bear our cross just as He empowered His Son to bear His. And when the agony of it seems beyond our capacity to endure, may we find comfort in these words from the Koran:

> From God there is no flight but only unto Him.
> Against a father's sternness no revolt avails.
> A child's sole refuge is within His arms.

13. Be Alive While You Are Living

Everything we have learned about life leads us to press as one of its major uses merely being alive while we are living. Live to the fullest while life is ours, is the wisdom the years have taught us.

Several cogent reasons prompt our urging this use of life. One is that life is so desperately short at any time. At best no one is long on this earth. Even those who live longest are on earth only for a second as God reckons time. A second compelling reason for living to the fullest is that life is always precarious and insecure and not least so nowadays when all mankind is living with the sword of atomic warfare suspended by a thread over its head.

One of our main reasons for commending being as fully alive as possible is the obvious recollection that for each one of us life grows shorter every day and that there is no time to waste if we plan to get in any vivid and consequential living before we die. The plain fact is that we just do not live forever here on this earth, yet countless people keep deferring exciting plans for living to some continually retreating tomorrow as if there always would be time. So often it happens that life passes these people by and slips out of their grasp before they have begun to carry out the dreams and plans they spent a lifetime postponing. The voice of wisdom says to the man who is always going to begin living tomorrow: "Live today for tomorrow may never come."

Above all other reasons, the fact that so few people are really alive commends this use of life. Recall how few people live with any visible evidence of joyous gratitude just because they are alive! We should wake up each morning with a song of thanksgiving on our lips that God has granted us another day of life, but how few of us do! Our waking prayer should be: "O God, who gavest me and all men life, help me to be alive this day and all the while I am living; for the sake of Him who gave eternal life to me and to all men." Such should be our daily prayer, yet most of us spend our days in whining and complaining, in fussing and fretting, never once thanking God for the gift of life and for another day to enjoy it. We can be sure that if we who are living do not appreciate how wonderful a gift it is just to be alive, they who are dead know. The pity of it, the tragedy of it, that we who are living do not realize the miracle of the privilege we enjoy!

Be alive while you are living, is one of life's imperious commands, and to obey this injunction is one of its paramount uses. Yet, even as we say this, we cannot avoid remarking how widespread among men is fear of life and fear of living to maximum capacity. We can understand a man's fear of death: it is an unusual man who does not dread this climactic experience of life and look upon it with apprehension and dread. Being an untried venture and a going forth into a strange region, we understand quite sympathetically their trepidation.

But we find it difficult to comprehend why men fear life and why they are afraid to be as intensely alive as they can be while they are living. Men fear life to such a degree that persons who are too intensely alive are considered just as dangerous as people who are either too good or too bad. The only thing to do with such people, society appears to say, is to get rid of them. This fact explains to us why among other reasons Jesus was crucified: He was too vibrantly and too vividly alive to be allowed to stay living.

This is a hard truth to become reconciled with, for to be alive is the obvious intent of life and, one would assume, the purpose of it. The central aim of life is living, yet why this fear of life, this reluctance to be as completely alive as possible while life is ours?

We suspect that many people hesitate to let themselves be fully alive because they know the price they will have to pay, suffering. In a way they are right, for there is a measure of anguish to be borne if we are too much alive. We will be misunderstood, called unstable and eccentric, and probably harder words than these. We will be tagged dangerous men in a world which combats every effort to alter or vary from the status quo. The world has its own way of handling too alive people: it crucifies them.

People are afraid of letting themselves be totally alive for they know the pain of being too responsive. It is an emotion-draining experience to look out upon the world and rejoice over its loveliness and beauty and then turn and behold its misery and sorrow and sin. Keen and vivid awareness of the beauty of life and the tragedy of it all but tears a man's soul apart within him.

Again, people are afraid of life, we suspect, because they know it is a violent and explosive force altogether too dynamic to let loose in a world they would like to keep on an even keel. The thing to do is throttle life, check it, inhibit it, dull it, kill it, anything, in short, but not let it run untrammeled and free. Keep it under cover, keep it in shackles, but do not let it escape from the prison in which it must be kept captive for the sake of safety.

Fundamentally, fear of life and fear of living at the peak of capability are due to a single cause: the deliberate refusal to accept life as a highhearted adventure in the name of God and for the sake of mankind. This is the heart of the matter: either we regard life as a high-souled adventure, trusting ourselves to some big scheme, and the bigger the better, such as God's dream for men, and so are completely alive while we are living, or we refuse to accept life in this spirit and so die years before we are officially declared dead. The option stands before us and we can choose the way our life shall go: we can live while we are living or we can die before we are dead.

We know full well that it takes strength to live and that a bountiful supply of vital force is necessary in order to move through our days as persons who are fully alive while we are living. But everything we have learned conspires to hammer home to us the wisdom of living brightly, expectantly, and joyfully while life is ours.

Who tries to be wholly alive while he is living is as brave a man as any courageous adventurer who set out to scale a cloud-capped mountain peak or any fearless explorer who sailed into uncharted seas. It takes a brave man and a man who is willing to learn more than most of us want to know for this assignment. It calls for a man who refuses to die before he has learned all that he can possibly discover while life is his. It calls for a man who loves this world while he is in it, a man who is alive while in this world because he loves it.

Beyond this, the man who is fully alive while he is living is apt to be a poet, not in the sense that he necessarily writes verse, but a poet in his touch on life; he looks upon life and living with rapture and wonderment and awe.

We are all poets in our youthful years. Our single duty in life is not to lose the awareness, the responsiveness to life, the startling capacity for joy and also for pain, the magic, so to speak, of those quickly sped days. Life's supreme tragedy is not poor health, lack of wealth or beauty or great gifts, a disappointing marriage, or having a boresome job to do, grievously hard as these may be to bear. It lies in the fading of our youthful vision, and our greatest sorrow is ever the death of that sparkling, water-clear spirit of wonder we possessed as children, that keen joy in the world and in all living, that pure faith and believing heart, that bubbling of the divine joy within us.

A simple, clear-eyed, and childlike sense of wonder precedes every good thing in life at every age, and it is the surest guarantee and pledge that he who possesses it will derive the maximum richness from every moment of living. He who has lost this quality of spirit is to be pitied: he may be alive but he is not truly living. The world, harsh as it is and hard as it may become, will always have a bounty of good things to offer him who keeps the spirit of wonder and awe forever burning in his soul.

The man who is all alive while he is living is also likely to be a mystic, and in using that term we mean simply a person who sees God's hand everywhere and in everything. A mystic is merely a person who opens his or her eyes and sees that the whole world is full of God. He or she is not peculiar, unbalanced, or nervously overwrought. Of all men, it may well be that the mystic is the most normal and sane.

The mystic is one who realizes more vividly than other men the vast significance of the element of mystery in life. He knows full well that "there are more things in heaven and earth than are dreamt of" in our cocksure, puny philosophies. He is entranced by the magic mysteries of common, everyday life. He is aware how unsearchable is the darkness out of which we have but recently stepped and how luminous is the life into which we shall presently pass. Of all men, the mystic, instead of being removed from life or insulated and isolated from it, is the closest to the very heart of life itself. Of all men, the mystic is perhaps the most sensitively alive, for he is almost agonizingly beset with a realization of "what an astounding thing it is, merely to live."

The unique thing about the mystic is that he is one who has fallen in love with God. He moves transfigured through a transfigured world, seeking traces of God everywhere and finding them wherever he goes. God, who is to some only a cold theory or an "oblong blur" or merely a metaphysical idea is to him a living presence and a constant joy. What is to some only thought is to him actual experience. What is to some only a probability is to him that which alone makes life worth living.

The man who is wholly alive is, above all other things, awake: just to be awake is to be alive and living. Awake and alive, responsive to the world, to life, and to God, such is the man who is completely alive while he is living.

"We die daily," said George Macdonald. "Happy those who daily come to life as well." Our prayer for those we love is that of Jonathan Swift: "May you live all the days of your life." And our advice to all is, in Seneca's words: "Begin at once to live, and count each day as a separate life."

14. To Die and Keep on Living

The man who aspires to be fully alive while he is living has assigned himself a task to challenge and test every resource he has within himself and that he can possibly muster. What commends itself as a worthy ideal is a vastly different thing to perform. That so very few remain through the years in love with life and firm in their resolve to be always and at all costs thoroughly alive indicates how hard it is to be glad for all that life brings.

He who loves life is most severely tested by tragedy and pain, disappointment and defeat. When these, one or all of them, strike him, he is called upon to demonstrate both the measure of his manhood and the skill he has acquired in wresting dividends from defeat, in transforming catastrophes into triumphs, in turning disasters into victories, in transmuting evil into good. To be overcome and vanquished yet not defeated is victory in life. How to win this victory is an art every man must learn or fail in living. And the earlier in life this art is learned, the better, for the harsh and crushing blows that seem to be a part of human experience come sometimes when a person is young, not always in the middle or later years.

Another way of expressing it is to say that every man must learn how to die and keep on living. Every parent who has left a son buried in the soil of some distant battlefield or who has stood by helpless as his child lay stricken with polio knows what is meant by that phrase. Every man who has witnessed the collapse of his dreams, every person who has stood by in numbed silence as his brightest hopes were cruelly shattered, every person who has beheld his private world crash in ruins about his head, every such person, be sure, knows what it is to die and yet be required to keep on living. And every such person will readily agree that one of the principal aims and uses of life should be to learn the secret of how to die and yet to keep on living.

Every man needs to possess this secret; every man will one day, sooner or later, have occasion to make use of it. Unless a man is living under some special dispensation of Providence, and we have not yet met a man who is, he will in the course of his years suffer blows of fate and fortune which can be described in no other way than catastrophes. What then?

We know well what happens. Either he is so beaten and overwhelmed that he never rises again, or by virtue of some power he possesses he is enabled, slowly but surely, to rise and stand erect once more. Either he fails or he wins. Either he is defeated in the battle of life or he proves himself a victor. Either he triumphs over life or life triumphs over him. It is one way or the other. There is no in-between.

Life offers no choice. Either a man masters the art of dying and somehow keeping on living or he fails to discover the secret that will equip him to deal victoriously with the devastating blows life deals all men alike. There is no sterner assignment in life than this, and here, if nowhere else, a man needs all God's grace that he can summon to his aid in order to achieve success.

To die and keep on living, how do we manage to do it? How do we even make a beginning?

By way of answer, first of all, we should pray God to keep us from bitterness and resentment and to preserve us strong in faith, when disaster rolls in on us like a tidal wave or crashes down on us like lightning.

To keep free of resentment when disaster strikes we must somehow get beyond blame. One way to do this is to regard our misfortune as a man views trouble, not as a child. When trouble or worse than trouble comes, our childish impulse is to place personal blame on some object or person. If we stumble over a stool in a dark room, we stop and turn and kick the stool, as if it were at fault for being in our way. And when we cannot single out a person to blame for our hurt, we curse God or whatever we look upon as the power behind the universe.

Mature men, however, seek always to understand and try not to blame. They see that evil is not directed vindictively at them. They are aware of certain laws operating in a larger sphere in which they happen to be involved. With the detachment and objectivity of maturity they move beyond their childish tendency to blame God or Fate for their hardship, striving to view their personal catastrophe from a long-range perspective, that is, in the light of all that they know about God's purpose and will. Thus they are enabled better to understand and to adjust to the new situation and by getting beyond blame to begin bringing good out of evil or grievous loss.

Few men can ever get completely beyond the inclination to blame someone or something when catastrophe strikes them low, but surely the more men can escape it, the less their faith will suffer in time of crisis or despair.

The second thing to do when disaster sweeps in on us is to realize that nothing happens to us as a unique experience leveled at ourselves alone by some special design of malevolent Fate.

Of course, when trouble comes our self-consciousness is heightened and our vision is apt to become warped. We think that we alone are called upon to suffer, to bear disappointment or loss, and that upon us only has evil fallen. But if we are mature people, we shall maintain our emotional balance and realize that others are suffering too and that countless others are in far worse plight. There is an Oriental proverb worth remembering when we feel self-pitying and resentful because misfortune has overtaken us: "I was without shoes, and I murmured, till I met a man without feet."

God is not petty or peevish or mean and certainly He is not cruel. In time of trouble, remember this, and also that God loves us with a love surpassing our knowing, despite any and all apparent evidence to the contrary. Christmas Day and Good Friday and Easter Day and Ascension Day should never let us forget this. Christ was born and died and rose again that we might know the measure of the Father's love.

A further step in redeeming a disaster is to discover during or after it what good values we can wrest from it, what advantages and benefits we can produce even from our loss or defeat.

It seems to be a law of life that only through the direct experience and patient endurance of pain we may come into knowledge of the wondrous secrets of God. Our destiny is glory, but the route we must travel to our goal is suffering gallantly borne. Our hearts must be baptized with fire and our wisdom purchased at the cost of sorrow and tears. Suffering and sorrow are the knives life uses to whittle off our sharp edges, but our spirits, if steadily enough whetted on adversity, in turn become knives "keen enough to challenge agony to yield life."

Spiritual development through disaster manfully endured —this is what we mean by wresting dividends out of defeat. Growth through the patient bearing of pain is another way of saying the same thing. Defeats, misfortunes, disappointments, setbacks, suffering—these are not things to be ashamed of. They happen to everyone alike and they are, if we handle them aright, literally the making of us. It is difficult to see it, but the blows we are reeling under right now may well be just what we need, as God views us, for our further spiritual development and growth into the full stature of real men. It must be said: we need all we get in life and we get all we need.

Never to be forgotten is a man who mastered the skill of how to die and keep on living, who possessed the secret of knowing how to draw abundant good out of bitter loss and shining victory out of black defeat. About every disaster that could befall a man struck him in a space of only a few short weeks. But in the midst of it all and though his eyes were yet blinded by their own tears he wrote a letter in which was this magnificent line: "My palace of dreams has collapsed, but I'm building a cathedral out of the ruins." Confronted by such a noble spirit the verse of G. A. Studdert-Kennedy comes to mind:

> Blessed are the souls that solve
>   The paradox of Pain,
> And find the path that, piercing it,
>   Leads through to Peace again.[1]

It is by the way it endures suffering that the soul bears witness to itself. By the way we bear our heartache and pain, by the spirit in which we carry our cross, we give notice to the whole world what our souls are. Courage, which Amelia Earhart described as "the price that Life exacts for granting peace," is not just to bare one's breast to receive the quick sword thrust. It is, rather, to feel "the daily daggers of relentless steel and keep on living." True courage is really to die and keep on living. He is a victor in life who surmounts his life's disasters by the nobility of his own manhood and by the help of God's grace and who, though he dies a thousand deaths in his heart, keeps on gallantly living.

> . . . One adequate support
> For the calamities of mortal life
> Exists, one only, an assured belief
> That the procession of our fate, howe'er
> Sad and disturbed, is ordered by a Being
> Of infinite benevolence and power,
> Whose everlasting purposes embrace
> All accidents, converting them to good.[2]

[1] "My Peace I Give unto You," from *The Sorrows of God*. Copyright, 1924, 1951 by Harper & Brothers.

[2] William Wordsworth, "The Excursion."

15. Obeying "Fate"

If one of the uses of life that the years press upon us as of primary importance for success in life is to learn the secret of how to die and keep on living, another is how to obey what men commonly call fate. By learning how to obey "fate" we mean simply that a man must master the art of going along cheerfully with what must be, with what appears to be for him the will of God. It is not the Greek idea of fate that we have in mind so much as the Christian concept of the will of God when we speak of "fate." Our meaning is best made clear by citing a sentence scrawled on the wall of a dungeon in the Tower of London: "The most unhappy man in the world is he who is not patient in adversities, for men are not killed by the adversities they have, but by the impatience with which they suffer." Agreeing wholeheartedly, we maintain that one of the paramount uses of life is that of a disciplinary school in which we shall learn how to endure patiently, how to bear hard circumstances nobly, or, put another way, how to obey fate, or the will of God, or what apparently has to be.

On the wall of another cell in the Tower of London there is still to be seen a verse in Latin of only four lines and eight words carved there by an unknown prisoner over four hundred years ago. Here are the lines and our rendering of them:

Deo servire	To serve God
Fato obedire	To obey fate
Poenitentiam inire	To be repentant
Regnare est.	Is to reign like a king.

Only four lines and eight words, but what a wealth of insight! "To serve God, to obey fate, to be repentant, is to reign like a king"—such is the wisdom of some anonymous dungeon prisoner of centuries ago who knew the secret we must make our own if we hope to succeed in living and if we aim to enjoy happiness and inward peace during our days.

To serve God, to obey fate, to be penitent—this is to reign like a king, we are told. To obey fate, to go along with what evidently has to be—*"Fato obedire"*—is the crux of the matter and just about the hardest thing we find ourselves called upon in life to do. The ability to acquiesce in what life deals out to us and to accept with a good grace all the harsh blows "fate" or whatever we call it sends to us is a capacity developed only by faith in the goodness of God that is required to approach almost heroic proportions. Mighty faith in God is needed for such obedience.

Yet the energy we waste in rebellion against the decrees of fate, or the acts of destiny, or the will of God, would be much more profitably employed in serving God by courageous and cheerful acceptance of our lot. We grow angry over the weather, which, of course, we cannot change. We eat out our hearts because we have been denied some talent or gift others we know share and possess. We sear our souls with the flames of envy because we lack a neighbor's charm or position or wealth. We crave strength that we might achieve great things and we resent bitterly that we are weak and can only accomplish little things. We want health that we may do exciting things and are angry because we are given infirmity and so can do only dull things. We yearn for riches that we might be happy and are incensed because we are poor in order that we might become wise. We want all things that we might enjoy life, forgetting that we are given life that we may enjoy all things. And so it goes. We do everything but obey "fate." To obey "fate" is the one thing we either cannot or will not do.

But is it not both better and wiser to go along with what evidently has to be? To obey "fate" is highest wisdom, we have learned, for therein lies the avenue to peace. *In la sua voluntate e nostra pace,* "In His will is our peace," declared Dante over six centuries ago, and rightly too for nowhere else is abiding peace to be found. The basis of all inner peace lies in the cessation of conflict between two wills— God's and ours—and it is our will always that must submit. When submission has been made, then and then only will peace come, a rare peace like "the stillness of an axis at the center of a wheel."

How do we come by the grace, the strength, needed to enable one to submit to God's will or what the non-Christian calls the decrees of destiny or the dictates of fate?

A stupendous confidence in God's benevolent purpose, in His providential love and care, is the first thing that will enable us to obey "fate," that will aid us to make perfect resignation to the divine will. To obey "fate" we must be armed with a majestic confidence in God's goodness and love, for only such a faith helps rebellion to die, bitterness to disappear, and courageous acceptance to come. Only by serving God with a shining, splendid faith can we begin to obey "fate."

Then there is prayer, the means and process, the discipline and so often the heart-tearing anguish, by which we struggle to get our wills in line with God's will and hold them there. The whole labor of prayer, we believe, should be directed toward this end—getting our wills in line with God's will, and, this achieved, through further prayer acquiring the strength to perform what God requires to be done.

Prayer is supremely the means whereby we get our wills in step with God's will. Prayer is not the futile endeavor of trying to pull God to us, but it is the effort and process of pulling ourselves to God. It is not primarily getting *from* God; it is essentially getting *to* God. It is not our vain effort to mold God to our desires. It is, rather, the lifelong effort to conform our will with God's desires.

On our knees strength comes to obey "fate." In and through prayer grace comes, the grace we seek, the grace we need to be able to accede to God's will and to obey what men commonly call "fate." Prayer, we have found, is the principal means by which we get our lives in harmony with God's will in the obeying of which alone we achieve contentment and any measure of inward peace.

Out of praying grace comes and peace, too. By means of prayer God bestows upon us what all men seek, His own peace, that marvelous peace that transcends and defies all human understanding. Out of prayer grace comes enabling us to obey "fate" and also, above all other gifts and rewards, "the deep and lovely quiet of a strong heart at peace."

A soul at peace with life, with the universe, and with God, issues from sublime faith in the goodness of God and from living closely with God in prayer. It results from bringing our wills into harmony with God's will and also from having our lives stayed on God, on what is eternally unchanging in the midst of constant change.

Every man's life is fixed more or less steadily upon one central point of attraction. It may be success in business or politics or warfare or letters, but every man's life is with varying constancy stayed somewhere. He alone attains anything like perfect serenity of spirit and peace of mind whose life is stayed on God, the source of all wisdom and light, of all power and love, in whom alone lasting joys are to be found. He alone can reconcile himself with "fate" whose eyes are firmly fixed on unchanging God and whose life is anchored in Him who is the rock of everlasting strength.

Finally, the possession of a soul at peace is the result, after long and patient striving, of coming to look on everything as God does, of seeing the whole cosmic scene and the outstretched life of all humankind as God beholds them. The objectivity of God—no less than this is needed to obey "fate" or God's will and thus to enjoy inner peace. God's rain and His sunshine fall on all alike.

Some rare spirits achieve "the deep and lovely quiet of a strong heart at peace" in youthful years. But for most of us this precious gift comes, if it comes at all, late in life. With the passage of the years our lives come to have a rather remarkable peace and an altogether curious power in them. We come to have in our lives what Wordsworth called "central peace subsisting at the heart of endless agitation." Of course, it may be just that we have at long last acquired what George Gissing called "the reasoned tranquillity of the mature mind." Yet, again, it may actually be that we have come at last into possession of that most wondrous gift of God, His own peace "which passeth all understanding."

The having of a soul at peace—at peace with itself, with other men, with life, and with God—by whatever means we achieve it and whenever during life we come into enjoyment of it, is our greatest asset as we make our pilgrimage through life on earth to God. By obeying "fate" or by making God's will our own, peace comes. But remember that even when it is won

> Peace does not mean the end of all our striving,
> Joy does not mean the drying of our tears;
> Peace is the power that comes to souls arriving
> Up to the light where God Himself appears.[1]

[1] "Studdert-Kennedy, "The Suffering God," from *The Sorrows of God*.

16. The Lesson of Obedience

Learning obedience to God's will, how to obey what men commonly describe as "fate," and by so doing to win the soul's peace brings us to the use of life as a school of obedience in every sphere and on every level if happiness in life is our aim and our desire. It is not just obedience to "fate" that we must learn in life, nor just obedience to our superiors and masters basically important as this is. We must learn how to subject our wills to facts (God's acts), to life's laws, and to God's commands. The only real way to dominate life is to obey it.

The facts about ourselves, these, first of all, we are required to obey. We may not like them, but we must respect them. We have to accept what we are and what we have and start from there. In life we have no choice but to shape our arrow out of our own wood.

To accept ourselves and our lot is one of the most difficult things we are called upon to do, but until we do it, happiness will be beyond our grasp. We are compelled to accept ourselves as we are, not as in our dreams we wish we were. We are required to accept ourselves not as finished products but as persons, each one of us, possessed of our own particular share of capacity to be and to do something fine and fair, and glad and good. And then the watchword is, Go to it!

Many people get panic-stricken when they find they are not so gifted or so well-favored as others. They forget God judges us by how far we have risen from where we began, by how well we have used the one talent granted us.

Other people spin into a twirl when they realize they are different from others, as if men are all alike, like clothespins in a basket or bananas on a stalk. Each of the twelve apostles was different from his fellows. Each followed his common master at his own gait and served Him in his own way. Each one did what he could for the cause, not what the other man could, and each helped mightily.

This is the first factor in the lesson of obedience life teaches us: cheerful acceptance of the facts about ourselves and the situation in which our service to God is to be rendered.

We must obey, next, God's plan for us; that God has a plan and a purpose for each one of us, we may rest assured. As Horace Bushnell preached, so we believe: "Every man's life a plan of God." God has a purpose for each of us, a work for every man to do, a place for each one of us to fill, an influence to exert, a likeness to His son for each of us to show forth, and, at the end, a place for each one of us in His Presence.

There is a plan working in our lives and fashioning them, and our earliest wisdom should be to trace its outlines and get our lives in harmony with it. Happiness flows from obeying the plan God has for our lives, while all manner of miseries stem from not living in accord with it. If we keep our hearts quiet and our eyes open, the elements work together; and, if we do not, they all fight together, and go on fighting till it comes right somehow, somewhere, and sometime. The plan works out; God sees to that. We obey the plan and know happy days, or we fight the plan and live sorry days, the dreary days men know who defy God's will.

Then there is that obedience to the laws of life and the demands of God we either make or pay the penalty for refusing. It is by violating one or more of these laws of the universe that most of us first learn of their existence. Though we are told in our school years that there are moral and spiritual laws which are as rigidly abiding as any laws of the physical universe, it takes most of us a long time to make this knowledge firmly a part of our life's wisdom. We are really mature when we discover that we must live in accord with them or perish and that we do not break these immutable laws of God but rather that they break us.

There are some things a man cannot do and live. Trying to live under water is one such thing. Another is trying to live in defiance of the moral structure of the universe. The laws of God are not statutes but realities. They are of the eternal and ultimate nature of things. We can violate human laws and escape punishment until we are caught. But not so with the laws of God. If we violate a law of God, we catch ourselves, and the punishment is automatic and immediate and inexorable. We do not break God's laws; they break us.

They who have learned in the middle years or late in life what they should have learned early and young are the most emphatic in stressing the use of life as a school in which to learn the lesson of obedience to the fundamental laws of the universe and of God. They have found to their sorrow and pain that if such obedience is not learned easily when young, it is learned the hard way, with severity, when old. They have discovered what no one of us should forget, that unless we discipline ourselves, the world disciplines us, and not with gentle admonitions but with harsh and staggering blows.

The laws of living with other men and with God, the laws of safety and sound health, in short all the laws and rules of life and living—of course, we do not have to obey them, yet maybe, after all, we do, or live in a state of perpetual torture, agony, and hell. Most people spend a lifetime learning this truth. When they have learned it, life's purpose, perhaps, is done.

Surely we know that "a free conscience is one of the greatest conservers of vitality that human personality possesses." If we live according to the rules, moral, physical, and spiritual, we will always be happy men and free, but if we violate conscience, spiritual misery is the result. We shall live a tortured existence if our conscience is clouded by guilt, if our mind is tormented by fears. Surely we know that we must obey conscience at all times and at every cost, if we would live happily. Keep conscience clear and clean and free and then every day is a joy to live, no matter what it brings, and no man will ever be able to hurt us.

To obey conscience is a large part of the obedience we must learn in life, for, in Martin Luther's words, "it is neither right nor safe to act against conscience." The wisdom of the ancient Hebrews echoes down through the years urging us, late and soon, to obey our inner voice and never to hurt our conscience with any known sin: "That which is altogether just shalt thou follow, that thou mayest live." George Washington's is the counsel of the years: "Labor to keep alive in your breast that little spark of celestial fire called conscience." If we do this and obey the motions of our conscience, happiness and joy that money cannot buy will be ours.

Obedience to God is the whole of piety and it is also the sum of wisdom. Life is a training school in this obedience; and if, at the close of life, when its fever is over and its work is done, we have not yet learned this lesson, the experience and travail of the years have indeed been all in vain.

Duties are ours, events are the Lord's. God calls us to duty and the only right answer to give is obedience: "Obedience is the one key of life." God calls us, God commands, and it is better to obey cheerfully than complainingly, and better to obey blunderingly than not to obey at all. The test of our love is not feeling, but obedience. George Macdonald strikes the right note: "Heed not thy feelings: Do thy work." Our success in living happily through our days depends upon how well we have learned one of the great lessons life is well used to master, obedience to fate and to facts, obedience to life's laws and, above all, to God's commands.

17. To Be Happy in Our Days

If we have learned obedience, the basic lesson life seems designed to teach, we are well along the pathway that leads to happiness. And to be happy is one of the legitimate aspirations we all can and should cherish. To be happy in our days is certainly a worthy and commendable way to use life.

Some people are always pleasant and cheerful, happy and content. By virtue of some divine endowment the gift of perpetual happiness seems to be theirs. Their presence is ever a joy and an inspiration, a glad benediction and a bracing tonic to our weary hearts.

But then there are others who seldom are happy. It requires a conscious effort on their part to smile: the faculty of being spontaneously happy just is not theirs. Nothing has power to shake the mantle of gloom from their spirits for more than a fleeting instant. Happiness is something they never know and, unless a miracle transpires with them, something they will never know. Some fault of temperament, some flaw of disposition, some curious taint in their inheritance, something, whatever it is, precludes their ever knowing happiness.

Here they are: some who are able to be happy no matter how harsh their lot and how hard their days, and some who never are happy no matter how favorably life proceeds for them. What is the explanation? Why is this so?

It is a matter of strength, we believe, of that strength for life with which a man must be equipped in order to enjoy success in living. It takes strength to love life, and the best of us need continual augmentation of our own quotient of strength for life to make the adjustments we are continually forced to effect and which we either make successfully or become casualties in living.

Strength is required for happiness in life, that rare strength that will enable us to wrest boons and benefits and even joy out of those experiences which crush weaker men. Beyond strength for life one further asset is needed: gratitude for life. The happy people are they who live with a sense of abounding gratefulness to God for granting them another day to live. If we go through life cursing the day we were born, happiness will forever be beyond our grasp. But if we live with gratitude, welcoming all of life and all it brings, happiness will never for very long escape us.

Most of us want to live happily, most of us try to be happy, and most of us fit into neither category, those who are always happy and those who are rarely happy. Silently and covetously we envy those who possess the secret that enables them always to be pleasant and cheerful, serene and content, and to ride happily above adverse circumstance. What can we do to help ourselves be more consistently happy people and to live happier days?

We can answer this query by suggesting that we keep in remembrance several important truths. The first is to recall what is easy to forget, namely, that happiness comes accidentally and also, as Nathaniel Hawthorne pointed out, it comes incidentally. "Make it the object of pursuit," he observed, "and it leads us a wild-goose chase and is never attained."

We cannot create happiness. It has to come spontaneously to be genuine, and the harder we look for it, the more elusive it is to find. Happiness and the faculty of always being happy are, ultimately, a gift from God. Happiness just falls out of the sky, perhaps all undeserved and probably at a time when such a boon seems least likely to arrive. For most people, happiness comes from the cheerful doing of their duty, in doing their job in life as faithfully as they can.

We shall not find happiness by chasing after it, a truth many jaded, pleasure-seeking contemporaries have forgotten, nor shall we find it by adopting a short-range view on life. If to be as happy as we can is one of our goals in life—and it is an aim of which we most certainly do not have to feel ashamed—then the long-distance view of life is our most reliable guide. For continuing content and not for the passing happiness only of the immediate, fleeting hour, the long-range perspective will help us immeasurably. First and last things, the really important and the not so important, distinguish themselves when we consider our lives as a whole.

Further, we can help ourselves to be more happy by resolving steadfastly to be ourselves, no matter what the risk or the cost involved. If happiness in life is our goal, at least as much happiness as a man may rightfully expect, then a primary duty is to be the individuals we undoubtedly are. "It is the chiefest of good things for a man to be himself," according to Benjamin Whichcote, a seventeenth-century English cleric, and we heartily agree. ". . . be what thou singly art, and personate only thy self" is the same counsel in the quaint words of Whichcote's contemporary, Sir Thomas Browne.

Happiness will never be ours if we try to be anything other than the persons we are. The poser and the pretender and the man who is afraid to be himself have cut themselves off from happiness, so, in Browne's words, "swim smoothly in the stream of thy nature, and live but one man." No man will know happy days until he learns to have the courage to be himself.

To be happy we must not only be brave enough to be ourselves, but we must heed the Orphic saying, "Become what thou art!" To be happy in life we must live the truth we know, we must follow the star our eyes have seen, we must be true to ourselves, and we must serve the purpose we know is ours. Either we do this, or live wretchedly and die embittered and frustrated men.

". . . follow your calling," urged George Borrow, "for however various your talents may be, ye can have but one calling; . . . follow resolutely the one straight path before you, it is that of your good angel; let neither obstacles nor temptations induce you to leave it; bound along if you can; if not, on hands and knees follow it, perish in it, if needful, but ye need not fear that; no one ever yet died in the true path of his calling before he had attained the pinnacle. Turn into other paths, and for a momentary advantage or gratification ye have sold your inheritance, your immortality."

Beautiful words these are from the pen of a colorful literary adventurer of nineteenth-century England but they are wise also and true. We shall heed them if happiness is our goal.

Again, we find happiness in our days if we have a purpose in life, a job to do. Kierkegaard said that "purity of heart is to will one thing." To us his words bear an additional meaning than their obvious one, namely, that success in life and happiness in our days flow from aiming at one thing and consistently directing our fire at that goal. "The man who fixes on something definite in life that he must do, at the expense of everything else, if necessary, has presumably got something that, for him, should be recognized as the Inner Fire. For him, that is the Gleam, the Vision, and the Word. He'd better follow it. The greatest adventure he'll ever have on this side of the grave is following where it leads." So speaks America's lastingly great poet Edwin Arlington Robinson.

To be happy in our days several guideposts should be kept in mind. One is this: seek to get and then to keep life in balance. By that we mean to get the four elements of life, work, love, recreation, worship, in equal proportion so that the design of our lives if it were made into a diagram would be a plus sign.

Another is to obey a piece of homely advice which we first heard from the lips of Dwight Morrow and which he described as "Rule No. 6." What the first five or subsequent rules of this eminent American were, we do not know, but we remember gratefully his "Rule No. 6" which is this: "Don't take yourself too seriously." It is a grievous mistake to reverse this rule, while to obey it is one guaranteed way to know greater happiness in life.

Still other suggestions to follow if we would be happy in

our own days are these: live at a slower pace and at a quieter tempo; go along with life, ride along with it, and by so doing discover for yourself the miracle that life has wings; work on the construction gang and not with the wrecking crew; mind your own business and let your neighbor take care of his, above all, let God take care of those big matters in life which are properly and uniquely His concern; finally, place your faith neither in man nor money nor machines nor civilization, but only in God and His righteous purpose and will.

So far as enduring happiness in life is concerned, it depends on discovering the direction in which God is moving and then changing the course of our lives to go along in the same direction with Him. By doing this we shall come to understand what Helen Keller meant when she said, "Happiness—its fundamental meaning is a free breathing of the soul."

The truly happy people are those who are at peace with themselves, with their neighbors, and with God. They who are happy in their days are the strong believers in the support and guidance, the goodness and love, the beauty and victory of Almighty God.

Fewer obligations rest upon us with greater compulsion than this, to live as happily as we possibly can. There is no kinder service we can render ourselves and no finer office we can perform for our fellow men than to live all our days as happily as, with God's grace, we possibly can.

18. To Acquire the Wisdom of a Contented Heart

Using our days for the happiest living we are capable of leads us to their next use, that of utilizing them to grow in wisdom or, as we think of wisdom, the faculty of being content in any weather cloudy or bright. This is making use of life to learn the beauty and to acquire the wisdom of a contented heart. St. Paul and every saint mastered the art of contentment and because of this we esteem them pioneers in the science of living, examples for ourselves to emulate.

A choice spirit of seventeenth-century England, Sir Thomas Browne, both a physician and man of letters, declared: "Life is a pure flame and we live by an invisible sun within us." Truly he spoke, for life is a burning flame and we do live by "an invisible sun within us." For no reason whatever allowing the sun within us to be dimmed or eclipsed permanently by any hardship or defeat is an accomplishment life is well used to achieve. High wisdom, indeed, is needed to succeed in this endeavor and skill surpassing what most of us possess. It is a sound use of time to employ it in acquiring this wisdom and in learning this skill.

Rich and deep wisdom is required if we are to live in a contented spirit and with a happy heart. The type of wisdom we need comes quietly and almost unnoticed with the passing of the years, a wisdom that is above what the world counts wisdom. It consists in being too wise to be worldly and overly intrigued with this world. It is that ripe wisdom which matures quietly and unseen in the person who lives close to the heart of things and who has seen the world and taken its measure. It is the distinctive attribute which marks the man who has come into developed manhood, the man who has lived fully and richly and now stands "a little sunburnt by the glare of life."

This high and fine wisdom, the kind that enables us in all situations to be content, comes to most men late in life. A few rare spirits are born with this wisdom in their hearts and know it even in youth, but most men acquire it in the waning of life, and then only as the reward for having endured trials by fire.

Each stage of life has its compensations, and the autumn and winter years hold abundant rewards for those who have weathered the storms of springtime and summer days. On the downslope of life the follies and blunderings and tempest-tossings of youth are over, the shattering struggles of manhood are finished, and the richest years are lived in peaceful spirituality, as close as human beings can approach, with the onflowing truths of life and of God, in quiet understanding and silent reconciliation. In youth we may perceive these basic laws, in manhood we meet them in head-on experience, and in the winter years we dwell in serene accord with them. Toward the close of life, when ends are drawing together, we know the truth about it. At this point peace comes for the soul, and wisdom and contentment come too.

To be wise it is not necessary or even desirable to know the contents of books, a commendable though vain aspiration on the part of any man. To be wise in this life is to hold in our hand the key that opens the door upon lasting contentment. We know of no more valuable employment of life than to use it to come into possession of this key. Highest wisdom is a very simple thing within the capacity of every man to enjoy. It is always to be content. It is, no matter how life goes, to live with a contented heart.

Wisdom is to live this day today. It is not to permit the years that have gone by or the years that are yet to come to concern us as we live the present hour. The past is gone forever, and it is to be committed into God's hands. The future is not properly our concern. Only this day is ours. Consummate wisdom is to live this day as if we should never die and to seize upon the present minute as if it were eternal.

Wisdom is to pass through the world free from fear of what tomorrow may bring. It is to harvest with a grateful hand the richness of the present hour and, buoyed by a healthy curiosity and open-hearted wonder, to go on day after day to discover what further God holds in store for us. The surprises of life are truly the beauty of it. The mystery of what tomorrow may bring compels us to remain optimists and to be hopeful for the future no matter how somber a day today may be. Wisdom is to cherish the joy and beauty we have known and now know, and expectantly to await what follows upon the morrow's dawn.

It is indeed wisdom to treasure all the happiness in life that we have known, for all the joy, all the careless, wind-free gaiety, and all the happy hours we have enjoyed will be as a fortifying bulwark in days of different color. Whatever it is that fills life's cup high and full, it is not length of days, nor sum of possessions, nor even the world's bright honors. What makes life something so dearly prized that we regretfully, nay, forcibly, surrender it at the hour of death is the memory of those moments of sheer happiness when we held a cluster of stars in our hands. Moments such as these are not once lived and then speedily forgotten. They lend a tone, impart a melody, and bestow a fragrance on all the days that follow. Such moments have beginnings, but never endings: they do not die, for true happiness "is once to have touched perfection." In very truth, "the days that make us happy make us wise."

Theoretically, the Christian, whether old or young, has no problem at all so far as inner contentment is concerned, for he knows it is his duty to live with a contented heart, no matter whether the skies be dark or fair. It is the Christian's duty to be happy always—it is just as simple as that! When life goes rough and hard, the Christian is not just to be free from complaint and stoically brave and enduring. No! He is to rejoice! However constant his bearing of a cross, his life is to be a continual expression of joyful thanksgiving to God for His unspeakable gift, the gift of Himself in His Son. Because of this gift and because of the secret he knows— that God is Victor over evil and Sovereign over all—the Christian is always to be content, at all times to rejoice.

But Christian or not, it is a high art for any man to live on the level of ever-abounding happiness and abiding content. The grace of God is called for here, and a wisdom that exceeds what most of us have achieved. For wisdom, "a dawn that comes up slowly out of an unknown ocean," is for most of us knowledge and certainty we possess after they are too late to do us much good. Wisdom is then to keep sweet in spirit and not to allow bitterness to ravage our hearts or cynicism to corrode our souls.

The beautiful souls of the world, the people we never forget, know some mysterious art, some saintly alchemy, by which bitterness is converted into kindness, gall into gentleness, disasters into triumphs, ingratitude into benefits, and insults into pardon. If we would be content and know abiding happiness, then we must covet this science and learn this art. It is indeed a wise use of life to learn the secret of a contented, that is, a wise heart.

19. How to Live

As the main purpose of life is living, so one of the principal aims of living is to find out how to do it.

This is no short-term operation. Some discover early what others find out late, but for most men a whole lifetime is required even to make a beginning of learning the secrets of living and a tiny measure of the ways of God. It is a long and humble business, finding out how to live, and doubtless so because few of us obey God even if we listen to Him. It takes a full lifetime to bring us close to God and ready to die. When we have finally acquired some measure of understanding and insight about how to live, life's purpose then is done and we are ready to commence its final experience, that solitary adventure into eternity which begins with death.

What is the wisdom the years teach about how to live? In what manner do the years counsel us to live, if we would live to the uttermost while life is ours?

All that has been written in the preceding pages supplies our answer to these questions, but is there anything more to be said? We believe there are five things more. The first is to live affirmatively, that is, in the light of and by the strength of definite affirmations and positive convictions that make up our heart's wisdom regarding the meaning and use of life. We must "accentuate the positive and eliminate the negative." By so doing we turn the key that opens the door to the good life.

It is really a matter of getting one's grammar right, as Bowdoin College's distinguished president, William DeWitt Hyde, pointed out. "Live in the active voice, rather than in the passive. Think more about what you make happen than what is happening to you," he advised his students. "Live in the indicative mood rather than in the subjunctive. Be concerned with things as they are, rather than as they might be. Live in the present tense, facing the duty at hand without regret for the past or worry over the future. Live in the singular number, caring more for the approval of your own conscience than for the applause of the crowd."

No one cares what we do not believe. All that matters to ourselves and to other people as well is what we do believe, and what we believe is made clearly manifest by the way we live. By a man's actions we can define his creed. It is by our affirmations about life, it is by what we believe to be right and true and worth while, that motive power for living a useful and significant life springs. Some people, of course, do not believe this: their credo seems made up of negations. But we have yet to meet a man who is living a happy, constructive, and joyous life who lives by such a code. "A happy life is not made up of negatives," Walter Savage Landor reminds us.

How to live? The years instruct us, second, to live with courage, with compassion, and with thankful and loving hearts.

Courage is the first virtue of life as kindness is its final joy. It is the essential prerequisite for a successful pilgrimage through life, and compassion and kindness go along with it side-by-side. A brave heart is required that we may not be overthrown by disaster, and courage that we may so deal with events that our fellows may be made stronger by our example. The witness of a man standing-up to life in a courageous spirit does more for other men than volumes of moral exhortations or a lifetime spent in listening to pious sermons.

And live with a loving heart, for what the world needs is not dialectic nor ideologies but simply people with God's love in their hearts. Only love can heal our broken world and make it whole again. St. John of the Cross tells us that when the evening of this life comes, we will be judged on love. Life is a dark and a not too happy journey for most people, as possibly it may be for ourselves, so be swift to love, make haste to be kind, and, come what may, hold fast to love. Doctor Johnson believed, and the years have taught us the same truth, that "to cultivate kindness is a great part of the business of life."

How to live? The years have taught us, in the third place, to live with holiness and passion and joy.

As He who has given us life and called us into His service is holy, so must we aspire to holiness if we would one day see the Lord. There is far too little holiness in our world today and the world needs desperately the salt of holy living. Churchmen who should be "holy in all manner of living" are not criticized these days for being too holy: they are censured and scorned for not being holy enough.

Without a burning desire to become holy we shall not see

God. We may not share a flaming ambition to be saints and we may not covet the wearing of a halo, but if we propose to use life as a quest for increasingly deeper knowledge of God, we must aspire to holiness or abandon our quest before we start.

The years instruct us to live with passion, for life without passion is an insipid and vapid thing. Pity is all we can offer him who lives without enthusiasm and ardor, without passion and zeal. Home-upbringing, church membership, and education have all failed miserably if the young grow up to maturity without having enthusiasm for something high and great and fine kindled in their breasts.

Men who make a mark in the world are men who are fired by passion. Their goal may be wrong or false or it may be worthy and good, but it is the passionate zeal with which they serve it that causes their names to be remembered. Even today churchmen pause to honor the great heroes of the Christian faith, the apostles and saints of bygone years. They were ordinary men who became extraordinary men because of their towering faith, invincible conviction, and unfaltering devotion to their Lord. Shame be on us, their descendants, who allow the faith's enemies to win victories every day because of our indifference and lack of passionate dedication to God's cause! G. K. Chesterton once remarked that "Christianity even when watered down is hot enough to boil all modern society to rags." Think what Christianity could do for our confused and sorrowing world, if its adherents believed it and preached it and lived it in the full power of its hardly tapped potential!

The years further teach us to live with joy—joy which is the echo of God's life within us.

It is well for us to remember, those of us who consider life a high adventure with the vision of God its final goal, that people gaze on us to see the radiance they themselves have lost. They look to us, who are in no way exempt from those things that crush their spirits, to see if we have any secret that makes our souls unconquerable. But if they find us petty or complaining, or fretful and given to a sense of defeat, lackluster and without joy, they turn sadly away. We shall help win men to God only by a gospel of joy, and such a gospel it is the Christian's duty to live and his unceasing joy to preach. Mankind will listen gladly to those who love God passionately and with delight, to those who have within themselves a happiness that brings forth laughter and begets courage, to those who share the liberty that is born of a sure and certain faith, to those who find religion not weight but wings.

How to live? The years press upon us, fourth, the merit of living "as though we were always on the eve of the great revelation," to use Maeterlinck's phrase.

To live in this manner is to live with bright hope and eager desire and in tingling expectation of something wonderful yet to be. It is to live in a great spirit that we may be ready for a great occasion. It is, further, to live with a forward look and with a forward thrust. It is, above all, to live in a state of being ready for death whenever it may come. It is to live as a Vermont housewife said she kept house, in dying order. And this is no morbid way to live, be well assured. It is, instead, the most sensible, for every day the residue of life grows shorter. So live, the years advise, that we will be prepared for death, the great and final revelation, whenever it comes. Our cue, therefore, is to delay no longer in getting our lives right with ourselves, with our neighbors, and above all with God; in getting our relationships on every level in good order and keeping them there.

The years counsel us to live as on a mountaintop and to live with all our might while life is ours, to live as if this day were to be our last and to deal with our neighbor as if this day might be his last, to live, in short, as if we were standing even now on the threshold of the ultimate revelation. If we live in this manner, we can be sure that we will be wondrously alive all the days of our lives.

One final suggestion about how to live needs emphasis. It is that we should live as men who know that Easter Day has happened.

The early Christians knew and preached and lived one overmastering truth, the fact of Jesus' Resurrection. He who was dead and buried had risen from the grave into new and more glorious life and was alive and living forevermore! In the power of this imperial fact the early-day Christians lived and conquered and died. In the dynamic supplied by this gigantic certainty they lived with joyous radiance and died without fear in their hearts.

Why, then, do we live, so many of us, as if Easter Day had never happened? as if God had not won decisively the supreme victory over all the forces that militate against happy life for men? Do we not know that Easter really happened? or is it that we just cannot bring ourselves to believe such marvelous good news?

Whatever the answer, all our experience dins into our ears one great message: not to forget the wonderful good news of the Christian faith, the glad tidings that God has won the victory over all the powers of evil and darkness, and over death and sin; that Easter Day actually happened; and that Jesus is risen from the dead and is alive forevermore as mankind's heavenly priest and triumphant King of Kings. Easter Day has changed the whole face of things, and the world has never been the same since, nor can it ever be again what it was before it occurred. Let us, then, so live as men who know this is a world in which Easter Day could occur and, glorious to say, actually did happen.

Reduced to a sentence, the years' wisdom about how to live is this: Live as if Christ had died only yesterday, as if He had risen only this morning, and as if He was coming back to earth again with the rising of tomorrow's sun.

20. How to Die

Equally sensible as using our lives to learn how to live
is to use our days to find out how to die. Since each one of
us is going to die someday—no man gets out of this world
alive!—it would seem that to use our days to evolve some
reasoned philosophy about death is a purpose for life no
man can afford not to fulfill.

Yet, as soon as we say this, we know the instant reaction.
Of all unpleasant and distasteful subjects to talk about,
even to think about, death is foremost. We do not like anything associated with death and we shy away from even dis-
cussing it. Be that as it may and though we do not relish
the thought, we are, all of us, dying men. Each day we live,
we move one day nearer to that last event of our earthly
careers which now we dread even to think about. For ourselves, we do not see how we can avoid using life to find
out how to die.

Though we can understand why, rightly or wrongly, men
avoid death and thinking about it, it is curious and strange
that this attitude should be so prevalent. Certainly we all
know that we shall not escape death and that each one of

us must do his own dying. Surely we all know that one day each one of us will be called upon to meet death face-to-face. Even so, if we are like other men, we keep postponing what we regard as an ordeal—sitting down with ourselves and getting our thinking clear and straight with regard to this ultimate act and experience of every man's life.

Why men are reluctant to face up to death and why they avoid the subject by every means they can is not hard to discover: most men are afraid of death. The very word strikes terror into their hearts, or at least bitter dismay. In spite of everything we say or do, in our innermost hearts we are, most of us, frightened by death and dying. Quite naturally, we dodge the subject and seek to avoid any dealing with it or even thinking about it as much as we possibly can.

During the height of the carnage of World War I, in the winter of 1918, the Chief-of-Chaplains of the American Expeditionary Force, Bishop Charles Henry Brent, wrote: "It is our duty to look at the unfearful side of death." But is there such an aspect to death? we ask, recalling the words of Peter Finley Dunne who said in an article written shortly after the *Titanic* went down in April, 1912, "Any man who thinks at all is afraid of death."

We believe that there is an unfearful side of death and we know that it is the Christian faith alone that enables us to view death unafraid and to face it without terror in our hearts. It is a good use of life, we maintain, to see if we cannot make this Christian attitude toward death our own.

Not in fear but in confidence does the Christian die. He dies trusting utterly in the love and mercy of the Father-God. He is able to do this—entrust his soul to God for all that lies ahead and beyond—because he has learned in life the great lesson of trust in God.

Obviously, whether you or I will be able to entrust ourselves to God when death is upon us depends upon whether we have learned during life to trust completely in God for all of life, this life and the life to come. We most certainly will not be able to use words of calm trust in the hour of death if we have not become accustomed to using them in the preceding years. While faith's last work on earth is to carry us through the valley of the shadow of death when evening comes, it is in the morning of life that we must learn to lay ourselves quietly and without fear on God's wings. We must be well practiced in trust so that when the last hard flight is before us we shall have faith sufficient to carry us confidently through the portals of death.

But how do we arrive at the point where trust in God supplants fear in connection with death? Our answer is: by seeing the unfearful side of death, by viewing death as Christian faith enables us to look upon it.

In order to regard death in this light, that is, without terror and dread, a frank recognition of the entirely normal and natural character of death is the first thing that will help us.

Death is not something hostile to life or something apart from it. It is part of life and it is simply, and no more, its last event. It is, apparently, the next thing we need when we have finished here. All this life leads up to it. It just begins that part of life which lies beyond our sight.

So we regard death, whenever and however it comes, a perfectly natural and normal event in our life's story, like being born, and, like birth, just as necessary, and again, like birth, a sort of boundary experience. We make too much of it, really. It is only a watershed, a landmark, which divides life here from life there. It is the horror and fear of dying that is our chief trouble in regard to death, for in itself death is merely an incident in life, not a break, and most certainly not the definitive termination of it.

In order to gain a healthier attitude toward death, it is helpful, second, to remember that there are far worse things than death.

To live as a slave under a tyrant because one was not man enough to die fighting that all men might live free is far worse than death. To live in dishonor, cowardice, or disgrace, is far worse than death, too. Ancient Britons believed this, for in *Beowulf* Wiglaf says, "Death is better for every knight than ignominious life." Shakespeare's Claudio felt death to be "a fearful thing" yet the sentiment is only uttered, one suspects, to enable the poet to respond through the lips of Isabella, "and shamed life a hateful." Hopeless mental illness, interminable sickness, excruciating pain without surcease, disability beyond hope of reclamation—these are to many a man's way of thinking far worse things than death. The words of a wise man of ancient Israel come to mind: "death is better than a bitter life or continual sickness."

Recalling the Christian belief that "the greater and better part of life is out of sight" will help us also to adopt a less fearful view of death.

Judging by creed and conduct, out of sight means for many people nowadays also out of mind. But not so for the Christian, who believes that those he has "loved and lost awhile" are simply passed into a sphere of life which lies beyond his sight. Though out of sight, they are not out of mind. Invisible ties bind that world to this and this world to the one we cannot see.

The Christian concept of life as a pilgrimage from God through this earthly life to God again is another factor which will aid us to view death unafraid and dying without fear.

"Here we have no continuing city, but we seek one to come" is the Christian's byword, for the Christian considers himself a stranger in an alien land and a pilgrim journeying through it to his true fatherland and home, life with God in heaven. Life, as the Christian understands it, is a matter of all eternity, not just the years, however many or few they may be, that he spends on this earth. From God he has come and, after this life is done, to God he returns, is the Christian's faith. Death, to him, is simply entering the next phase of life which in turn will have as its ultimate end the vision of God in heaven.

If we can make this view of human destiny our own, we shall help ourselves wondrously in coming to a less fearful view of death. And, further, if we examine what the Holy Bible has to say about death, we shall be strengthened in our ability to regard dying without fear.

The Holy Bible refers to death as a going to rest, a going to sleep, when "the evening comes, and the busy world is hushed, and the fever of life is over, and our work is done." Jesus said, "Our friend Lazarus sleepeth . . . ." When Stephen was stoned to death, it was said of him, "He fell asleep."

Death is also described in the Holy Bible as a going forth from a land of bondage to a realm of liberty, as an act of liberation and emancipation freeing us to go forward into the promised land.

St. Paul presents a third Biblical view of death as a setting out to sea, an unmooring—"The time of my unmooring is at hand."

A fourth Biblical view of death is that of a going home after being wayfarers and strangers in an alien land.

The book of Genesis says death is a punishment and science tells us that death is just a law of nature. But Jesus shows us that death is a gate through which we pass into immortal life. According to the one person who lived on this planet and after death returned to this life, death is simply the gateway through which we pass to our joyful resurrection.

Add it all up, what the Holy Bible has to say about death, and we are mightily fortified in our effort to win and maintain an unfearful view of death.

The nature of that life into which we move at the instant of death is another reason why men can and should regard death without dread. "Eye hath not seen, nor ear heard, neither have entered into the heart of man, the things which God hath prepared for them that love him." So St. Paul believed and another great believer of a later century shared the same belief, William Law, who said that "the greatness of those things which follow death makes all that goes before it sink into nothing."

To the man of Christian faith the life beyond the grave is no gray and bleak no-man's land or a land of fearsome terrors. It is a life in which there will be a continuation of the best of this life. It is a realm where people will be found and where people will recognize one another. There will be a second chance for all and hope even for the ungodly. In Fiona Macleod's words, "Death is the keeper of unknown redemptions." Everything about the life ahead will appeal to our higher natures. There will be change and progress, development and growth. Life beyond the grave will not be an unending celestial vacation, but a life of realization and fulfillment. And there the servants of God will still receive God's blessed ministrations. "The souls of the righteous are in the hand of God, and there shall no torment touch them," wrote the author of the apocryphal Wisdom of Solomon. The former Dean of St. Paul's, London, W. R. Inge, echoes those ancient words in stating his conviction that "the souls of the righteous are in the hand of God, and what is dear to Him will never be plucked out of the land of the living."

Above all else, it is the Easter faith which enables Christian men to face death without fear. In this faith Christians joyfully live and peacefully die, for it is this faith alone, firmly held, which equips a man to die unafraid.

The event of Easter Day tells us that death does not mean what most men fear, namely, the destruction of self and the obliteration of personal identity. Jesus lived on after death as Himself, and His experience will be ours. Because He survived death, so also shall we. Because He lived on beyond the grave as Himself, so likewise shall we. As He retained His personal identity after death, so also shall we. Easter Day does not mean just that we shall live on after death. What Easter Day demonstrates and proves irrefutably to Christians is that we shall live on after death as ourselves, that our survival will not be as a drop of water in a pail of water but each one of us as himself.

Can anything more be said? Yes, one thing more, quoting Theodore Roosevelt from the book he wrote after his son Quentin was shot down over France in July, 1918: "Only those are fit to live who do not fear to die."

It is only the man who is not afraid to die who is free to live. The sky is his to hold in his hands, and the earth is his and all the richness therein. He alone is able to ride through life as on an eagle's wings.

Only when we are no longer afraid to die do we truly begin to live. When we have died to death, then life begins. When we have conquered the terror of death and surmounted our dread of dying, then we shall be as men born again. Something else too: we shall no longer be afraid of anything on earth or in heaven. When fear of death is overcome, all other fears instantly melt away.

Death holds no terrors for the true in heart. Death terrifies only the man who is afraid of life and who has not made of life a friend and of the God of Time and Eternity a trusted companion.

21. Winning Our Souls

Summarizing all the uses of life we have suggested stands the use of life as a God-given chance to win our souls. This seems to many people not only the best use that can be made of life, but the ultimate use. Back of this conviction that life is to be used for the winning of our souls stands the belief that while we have souls, we shall not possess them unless we win them.

Saint and sage and Son of God agree that life has meaning and worth only when it has reference to the soul, the soul's unfolding, its progress, and its growth. St. Francis of Assisi looked upon the people gathered to hear him preach not as men and women and children but as a company of human souls. Socrates urged his pupils, old and young alike, not to take undue thought for their person or their property, "but first and chiefly to take care about the greatest improvement of the soul." And Jesus of Nazareth looked upon men primarily as souls, as souls capable of becoming all that heaven is.

This is especially interesting nowadays for people are curiously reluctant to talk about the soul. They are actually embarrassed to be told they have souls and that their souls are their most notable feature. But we are, each one of us, more than just a body and a mind, reason and will, emotions and affections. Each one of us has a soul, is a soul. The innermost core of every man, the soul is that part of us which came from God, indwells our bodies here on earth, and goes on to God when life is done. The soul is the real, the essential, the indestructible, the eternal, part of us.

Jesus Himself spoke of the soul as if it were something that a man has but does not possess unless he wins it. Further, He told us how a man comes into possession of his soul—"In your patience ye shall win your souls." As we understand His words, Jesus was telling His disciples that, though they had souls, the soul, like every gift worth having, must be won by dint of effort and labor, prayer and desire, and at the cost of blood and sweat and tears. When He dares us to follow Him in discipleship, Jesus challenges us to embark on the quest of winning our souls. To win our souls, a prize so desirable and worth while that the world were well lost in order to gain it, is what Jesus summons us to do when He calls, "follow me."

How do we do it?—how do we win our souls?

We have already suggested several of the steps that are essential: learning how to die and keep on living, mastering the lesson of obedience, discovering how to maintain midst life's fever and ferment a contented heart, finding out how to live and also how to die. But more steps are necessary.

The first is to regard life henceforth if we have not done so before as a God-provided opportunity for growing a soul, or, as Robert Browning said it, "our chance of learning love." Life is the framework in which we are to grow a soul,

and not life as we wish it were but life as it is, the conditions of life and the world as they are. John Keats described the world as a "vale of soul-making." So we are to
consider this life; and either we accept the world as the
arena in which we are to make and grow a soul, or we can
make no sense at all out of our being here.

It does not appear from the evidence at hand and from
our experience of life that we are on earth just to have a
gay time, to make money, to win fame and applause, or to
capture the world's transitory honors and enjoy its fleeting
glories. If the world were designed for man's joy and happiness, something most certainly has gone wrong with it, as
the Christian faith insistently maintains has happened. And
if the world were meant for men's amusement and ease and
comfort, then it is a cruel and bitter mockery indeed. But
if it were designed to be the ground and sphere in which
men could fashion, each for himself and by God's help and
with private fear and inner trembling, an immortal soul,
then the world makes sense in high degree.

It is important to get this one thing clear, namely, that
our purpose in being on this earth and in this life is to grow
and develop in our hearts and bodies and minds and pre-
eminently in our souls. To grow a soul is our main business
here.

If the first step in winning our souls is to accept this
world and life as the arena in which we are to make and
grow a soul, the second is to accept cheerfully all that comes
to us in life as the raw material out of which we are to
fashion our immortal souls.

Now this, freely granted, is no easy thing to do—to welcome with open arms all that life has given, is now giving,

and tomorrow may give; to embrace gladly all the care and trouble, all the pain and sorrow, as well as all the gladness and joy, life sends our way. We may well be forgiven for wincing under the blows life deals us and well may we hope to be forgiven for seeking to avoid and escape further heart-break and pain if we have already had what seems to us our reasonable share, but we do so at our soul's peril. The soul requires for its growth all that is our destined experience of life. And we may rest assured that we shall get our appointed share of experience of life sooner or later. We shall not get more than our share, but we shall get our share, and the soul requires it all for its proper development and growth.

In life we get what we need and we need what we get. We are forced to believe this, if we elect to stand with those who count one of the great uses of life the winning of our soul. The measure of us and the only accurate gauging of our true worth is how we handle what comes to us, as to every man, and what we make out of it all. It is faith's noblest work ever to challenge loving-kindness out of all the roughest strokes of God.

Life is not meant to be easy: it is meant to be heroic. God never intended to make life an unending holiday for men: God means to make men great. We become great and we become men by taking all that life gives and brings and does to us and using it as the raw material out of which, with God's help, we are to fashion our immortal souls.

Further, if we would win our souls, we must be succeeding in a daily effort to win mastery over them. We do this by establishing the ascendancy of the spiritual over the physical, the higher instincts over the lower passions, the finer self over the baser self. "He is blessed," wrote Thoreau, "who is assured that the animal is dying out in him day by day, and the divine being established."

The level upon which we choose to live our lives is all-important, for what matters so far as this world is concerned and also the next is not what we do, but how we live. If we aspire to win possession of our souls, we must elect to live insofar as we are capable on the highest level, the divine plane, according to God-given standards and the noblest ideals known to man. If we endeavor to live human life in the divine manner, we shall not fail to win our souls.

What remains to be done, if we would win our souls? Our master guide tells us directly: we must endure. "By your endurance ye shall win your souls" is how Weymouth translates Jesus' words. "Hold out stedfast and you win your souls" is Moffatt's rendering of the same verse. We must endure and let patience have and do her perfect work in us, for capacity for endurance is spiritual power and by its stern observance God has trained the finest souls.

Men commonly call Jesus "Master." Why? Because He took all that came to Him, endured it, and through it all kept sweet in spirit, faithful to the end, trusting God and loving men. By always keeping the finer self in control of the lower, the higher man in command over the lower man, and by patiently enduring, Jesus won His victory. By following His example, when our Gethsemanes and Calvarys descend upon us, we, too, shall win our souls.

These are indeed times which try men's souls, but it is in these very times that we are called upon to win or lose our souls. Many a man has lost his faith, if not his soul, by fretful impatience and by inability to endure. Not easily did John Milton learn in his blindness that "they also serve who only stand and wait." Nor is it any easier for us these days to live by the same truth. But the winning of our souls is at stake!

God's delays are not His denials and "by bravely enduring, an evil which cannot be avoided is overcome." We know that he conquers who endures, and the Bible tells us that the man who endures to the end is blessed and shall receive the crown of life. Make these truths part of your heart's wisdom and live by them, for it is not so much in its achievement as in its endurance that the human soul reveals its divine origin and testifies to its immortal grandeur.

Of all this world's prizes, the one most worth winning is the knowledge that we have gained possession of our souls. By regarding life as the God-given opportunity for growing a soul, by welcoming all that life brings and gives as the raw material out of which we are to fashion our souls, by establishing the mastery of the spiritual man over the physical man, and by endurance in trouble and patience in disaster, we shall win life's most coveted trophy— the real possession of our immortal souls.

Conclusion: The End of Life

"Keep thine eye fixed on the end of life," counseled Solon of Athens. But what is "the end of life"? What is the point of it all, the courage we have had to display, the care we have had to bear, the work we have had to perform, the discipline we have had to undergo, the tears we have shed? What is the end of it all, the goal toward which it all leads?

Answers to this question abound, and they vary with a man's philosophy and creed. They range from the view of the hedonist who holds that the aim of life is to have as gay a time as one can as long as one can to the notion of the Roman philosopher and statesman Seneca who maintained that "the end of being is to find out God." William Penn of Quaker fame believed that "the truest end of life is to know the life that never ends," while Dr. William Temple, the Archbishop of Canterbury who died midst the violence of the recent war years in London, held that "man's chief end is to glorify God and (incidentally) to enjoy Him forever."

Working toward our definition of what is the end of

life, we would say, first of all, that it is not to live for self alone, for private gain and selfish pleasure, but to be, in whatever measure we are able, builders of a fairer world and co-laborers with God in establishing more completely the reign of His law and love in the world and lives of men.

But life has an even higher and greater goal than this. The end of life is not just to do something, however noble and worthy and good. The ultimate purpose of life is to become something.

Truly, the end of life is not just to do something, regardless of how wonderful and worth-while our achievement may be. A life can be utterly wasted in just doing, and the more frantic our activity the more positive we may be that we are on the wrong track. For some strange reason we seem to think, most of us, that the quantity of our achievement is what counts with God, whereas it is always and only the quality that is important. Our aim should be to do less better rather than to do poorly more than we are really able to do well. "Activity is only beautiful when it is holy," Amiel reminds us, "that is to say, when it is spent in the service of that which passeth not away." Yet so many of us appear to think that any and all activity is praiseworthy in the sight of God, and the more we do, the greater the praise.

If we think the end of life is primarily to do something that will stand as a monument to our memory after we have gone, we are inviting disillusionment and courting heartbreak, for what then do we have left if in old age, as not infrequently happens, a lifetime's labor is wiped out overnight? What then do we have left other than the ashes of our dreams as dust in our hands? We really have left only what we have become in and through and because of the days of our years. What we have done is gone but what we are and what we have become remain.

The end of life, we firmly maintain, is not just to do something: it is to be and to become something. Anyone, within obvious limits, can do something, but not everyone can be something. Any man who desires can go on Christlike errands and perform Christlike tasks and deeds. But not every man, just for the asking or wishing, can be a Christian man. We need to be reminded of this, for most of us are likely to spend so much time doing good that we find little or no time to be good. Most of us have not learned, or perhaps it is just that we have forgotten, that to be is infinitely higher than to do; that to be true is to perform a higher and a more lasting service than to spread and teach truth; that to be pure in heart brings us nearer to God, does more for our fellow men, and bears a more excellent fruit, than a lifetime spent in helping others to be pure; that to be just is more splendid than to aid justice; that to be a Christian in our daily walk makes more disciples than to preach the Gospel with the tongues of angels.

The real end of life is so to live, so to labor, so to suffer, and so to die, that at the finish of our soul's pilgrimage through time and eternity we shall be granted the vision of God. That this boon, which we esteem the highest good, may be ours, we accept life as a highhearted adventure of body, mind, and soul, in growth in knowledge of God and things divine and God's gift of life to us as our chance to win our souls.

This is to say that we view the final end of life as the achievement of a character, such a character as will permit us to enjoy the heavenly vision at the end of our days. To fashion through the years and out of all they bring such a character as will enable us at the end of life to behold God —this is the true goal of life. To become increasingly a man who can day by day lay stronger claim to his destiny as a son of God—this is the purpose behind all the travail and discipline of the years.

Plato tells us in words which he reports as coming from the lips of his master Socrates that "the end of life is to be like God, and the soul following God will be like Him."

If "the end of life is to be like God" and if such should be the aim of all our striving, then the purpose of life is clear. We are here on earth primarily to grow and to grow up. We are here to increase daily in mental power, moral capacity, and spiritual vision and grace, and, the Christian would add, to grow into the full stature of a new man in Christ.

And if "the soul following God will be like Him," the use of life is plain. It is to take all that comes our way in the unfolding story of our years and use it for the development of our souls in the direction of becoming like God. By so doing our infinite reward draws near, the vision of God in His majesty and beauty.

If such is the true end and the all-inclusive use of life, then life makes sense to us, for judging by our experience of it everything works toward that end.

Just living our years makes us far finer, far stronger, and far gentler persons than we were. The things that happen to us make us humble, and quiet, and kind. Each day we speak more softly and with eyes more kindly smiling, because we are more completely understanding. The obligations and responsibilities we are called upon to assume, the burden of suffering and heartache we are compelled to carry, the joy we have known and the beauty we have seen, these all make of us slowly through the years new and different persons, more like the men and women God apparently intended us to be.

The years have a way of developing in us an understanding heart. Such a heart and spirit and touch on life is the fruit of years of living. In youthful years we are too eager, too strong, and too much in a hurry to practice the amenities of the understanding heart, but the years, as they roll by, teach us to be kind. Rather, the years have a way of breaking us into gentleness and of grinding us into tolerance and love. Just by living our years and by love and beauty and by sorrow and pain our hearts are educated. It almost seems that one of the great purposes of God is to bring about in us, His children, the birth of understanding hearts. We know this, at least, that the person who has an understanding heart is like God and that the person who follows God and obeys His will eventually comes to possess one.

It is something, indeed, to have undergone the process by which God molds us into the persons He evidently intends us to be. It is something to have wept as we have wept and to have labored as we have wrought. It is something, toward the end of life, to be able to laugh with God's laughter because we have first wept with His tears. It is something to have known "perilous ancient passions, strange and high" and to have journeyed through our days, both the dark and and the bright, loving life, and living it to the uttermost right to the end. It is something to have loved all good and beauteous things, God above all, and to have searched for them and to have adored them. It is, in truth, no small thing at the end of life to feel that one has proved his man-hood, "the proudest of all possessions to a man," that qual-ity, Francis Parkman tells us, "which, strong in generous thought and high purpose, bears onward toward its goal, knowing no fear but the fear of God; wise, prudent, calm, yet daring and hoping all things; not dismayed by reverses, nor elated by success, never bending or receding; wearying out ill fortune by undespairing constancy; unconquered by pain or sorrow, or deferred hope; fiery in attack, steadfast in resistance, unshaken in the front of death; and when courage is vain, and hope seems folly, when crushing ca-lamity presses it to the earth, and the exhausted body will no longer obey the still undaunted mind, then putting forth its hardest, saddest heroism, the unlaurelled heroism of en-durance, patiently biding its time."

"The glory of God is a living man; and the life of man is the vision of God." Centuries old yet fresh as today's news, these words of St. Irenaeus, the Greek bishop of Lyons, France, in the second century, express the profound-est truth we have learned.

It is something, in all honesty, to have been all through one's years "a living man," to have proved oneself in the fearsome adventure of life truly a man, to have won one's soul, and to feel, near the end of life, almost as wise as the stars, almost as old as the sky. "The glory of God," no less, is he who is "a living man."

". . .and the life of man is the vision of God." Yes, surely, that is so: to have caught the heavenly vision even dimly here on earth is to set a man's soul aflame with a fire which never goes out, and it is to begin to live in the here and now "the life that never ends."

What is the end of life? It is so to live that the world will be better because we were born, yet it is not merely to do something no matter how meritorious and fine and good. It is to become something, to achieve such a character as will enable us at the conclusion of our pilgrimage through time and eternity to behold the vision of God in His incomparable beauty and holiness and to dwell with Him in His heavenly home.

And the great use of life? It is to grow like unto God. It is to grow into such persons that we may, when our journey through the years is done, be partakers of God's heavenly kingdom.

In the words of François Villon, "In this belief I will to live and die."

Mr. Valiant-for-Truth Passes Over

After this it was noised about that Mr. Valiant-for-Truth was taken with a summons, and had this for a token that the summon was true, that "his pitcher was broken at the fountain." When he understood it, he called for his friends and told them of it. Then said he, "I am going to my Father's; and though with great difficulty I got hither, yet now I do not repent me of all the trouble I have been at to arrive where I am. My sword I give to him that shall succeed me in my pilgrimage, and my courage and skill to him that can get them. My marks and scars I carry with me, to be a witness for me that I have fought His battles who will now be my rewarder."

When the day that he must go hence was come many accompanied him to the riverside, into which as he went he said, "Death, where is thy sting?" and as he went down deeper, he said, "Grave, where is thy victory?" So he passed over, and all the trumpets sounded for him on the other side.

— JOHN BUNYAN, *Pilgrim's Progress*